BOUNCING BACK

BOUNCING BACK

Handling the Humor and Heartaches of Frustration

BRENT D. EARLES

BAKER BOOK HOUSE

Grand Rapids, Michigan 49516

248.4
EAR

For **Bret Kroh** and **Johnny Dyer**

Throughout the writing of this manuscript
these two dear friends encouraged me again and again
to bounce back.
This dedication is in appreciation
of the iron they have used to sharpen
my sometimes dull edge,
and for the hours of listening they have given.
Guys, I love ya.

Contents

Introduction

Frustration is no stranger to us. He has been our unwelcome guest in the best of times and in the worst of times. We have felt his presence when we kept our heads though all about us were losing theirs, and when we *lost* ours while others were *keeping* theirs. He has come to call during our moments of most impenetrable strength as well as our spells of despairing vulnerability.

There are so many causes of frustration that one volume could not possibly touch upon them all. Some of them are major splinters scraped into our skin from the "dailyness" of our cross carrying. We would prefer our crosses padded, at the very least. Then we could bear them more easily and use them for resting chairs whenever we grew weary. How prone we are to forget that the splinters that pierce us can never compare to the spikes that pierced the Lord. And yet, that does not make them less painful. They still hurt, but they also make fellowship with Christ on a deeper level possible. When we are without frustration we begin to think we need no help. Splinters make good reminders.

Some frustrations are like sand granules caught in the eye; they are small and insignificant, but irritating. And they lie upon the beaches of life just waiting to be swept up by an unexpected wind. They are the persistent cries of children, muffled only by the uninterrupted cadence of a phone ringing off the wall. They are the speeding tickets we get because it has been one of those days when everything was fifteen minutes out of synch, and we were hurrying to catch up. They are the mornings when the toaster gets stuck in manual overdrive and turns the breakfast toast into certified hockey pucks. They are your husband's muddy bootprints on your freshly waxed kitchen floor. They are your wife's panty hose draped across the shower entry and getting wrapped around your neck at 5:30 A.M. as you climb into unusually scalding-hot water to wake you up. And, as you know, sand pebbles are countless.

Frustration is legitimate. I think that needs to be said here at the beginning or readers might get even more frustrated. It is a normal human response that God occasionally uses as part of his alarm system to alert us to problems, dangers, or much-needed changes. Frustration, though familiar, does not make a good friend. He is too unsettling, too aggravating. That he visits at all is enough; but if he sets up residence, serious action needs to be taken.

When I was searching for a clear definition for frustration I heard a speaker say, "Many Christians wrestle with life; they toss and turn and often get pinned. They muddle through but don't know what to say or do about the intense turmoil boiling down inside. So they accept living in a quiet desperation, never able to find a way to cope with the personal agonies they feel, whether those agonies be great or small." Two words—*quiet desperation*—sum it up.

Because frustration is hard to express, and because we are afraid no one will listen or understand, we tend to keep it to ourselves. But we grow desperate. "How long can this go on?" we ask ourselves. "How much more can I bear?" We reach for God but do not feel his presence. We get angry, or sad, or lonely, or hopeless, or defeated, and sometimes all of the above. We throw up our hands; we cry; we mope around; we pretend to ignore it; we sleep too much; we overeat; we pray routinely; we daydream; we feel caged— all signs that frustration is overstaying his welcome.

As the splinters are driven unbearably deep, we are wounded to our very inner core. Our true fiber is about to appear. We are forced to see ourselves as painfully weak and frail. Thrice we pray for God to remove this thorn, but he does not. We rub our eyes, stinging with sandy misery. Quietly, desperately, we whisper to ourselves, "Meaningless! Meaningless! Utterly meaningless! Everything is meaningless!"

Inked upon the lines of Ecclesiastes are the frustrations experienced by us earth-dwellers. You will find each chapter introduced by words from this Book of Frustrations. It should be remembered that a good deal of Ecclesiastes is told from a strictly human perspective apart from its spiritual insight. They are the words of fatalism told sarcastically by the writer to become "goads" and "nails" (Eccles. 12:11) for the readers. The message is loud and clear: whenever we get trapped in the tangled webs of life, all of life seems fruitless and worthless.

Now, let's get out the needles and tweezers and Visine and see what we can do about removing the splinters and sand.

1

Coping with "Rut-tine"

What has been will be again, what has been done will be done again; there is nothing new under the sun (Eccles. 1:9).

Semper eadem. It is the unspoken motto of the masses. Although they find dread in it, they cannot break free of its nagging, pawing grip. Translated from Latin it means "ever the same."

So it is for those stuck in the groove of broken-record living. Day after monotonous day of the unchanging routines of life is all they have to hope for. Life has become predictable, boring, and lackluster. Tomorrow holds no adventure, opportunity, or challenge for them. Occasionally— but only occasionally—they dream about what they wish life could be. But they never expect the slightest bit of it to happen. Frustration gnaws at their midsection as they wonder why not even one of the tiniest thrills felt by Indiana Jones comes their way.

Has this description tortured you enough? It is unpleasantly true of so many of us, isn't it? Just nod if any of these points strikes you. Or laugh. Or cry.

1. Do you think that you could walk through the rest of this week blindfolded—homelife, job, meals, per-

sonal habits and all—without a hitch, without so much as a scratch or stubbed toe?

2. Is the second most memorable day of your life the day you had a no-cavities checkup from the dentist?
3. Are the slides of your neighbor's trip to Iowa more exciting than your last three vacations?
4. Do you find yourself trying to memorize the answers on the back of *Trivial Pursuit* cards?
5. Do you eat your five "favorite" meals prepared in nearly the same order every week, with leftovers strewn in between?
6. Was the last time you learned a new word when you were taking the *Reader's Digest* Word Power quiz at the doctor's office over a year ago?
7. Do you go to bed every night at precisely the same time—at the conclusion of the newscast?
8. Are your daily devotions stuck in the mud?
9. Have you forgotten the last time *you* initiated a new friendship?
10. Do you scour every piece of junk mail, thrilled by it, even though you plan to trash it?

If you plead guilty to these boredom-barometers, perhaps your routine has faded into "rut-tine." You may be looking for a spark of freshness. What is more, you may be *needing* a touch of "newness" living. Those who never learn to take mini-escapes from the mundane often go over the wall when boredom completely imprisons them. They go AWOL from life, frustrated by the empty sameness of living devoid of challenge, triumph, and praise.

On the other hand, our society has become thrill-happy. The TGIF philosophy has permeated lifestyles and contributed to a more hopeless boredom for the week-long routine. Soon the reckless abandon of TGIF-ers doesn't wait until Friday to begin. With drugs or alcohol, "pep" can be had anytime. So it goes. Thousands get caught on a pleasure ride with inevitable unhappy endings. And why? Often because they want some spice in life and don't know where to find it.

So much of the walk in Christ hinges upon balance. Battling boredom is a good example. It is foolish to think life is supposed to be one great mountaintop experience after another. However, it is just as wrong to settle for a deeply rutted existence that never dares to enjoy the liberating freedom we have in Christ. There needs to be a happy medium—one that finds new meaning in daily rigors and, at the same time, is not afraid to step out onto the water with Jesus for a walk.

The New Wears Off

Solomon's futilitarian words ring a realistic message. Here is a man who had scaled the highest heights and plumbed the deepest depths. He had given nearly everything a whirl at least once. Now, with the voice of experience, he rises up to say, "New things soon become used; and exhilarating times eventually fade into duller adventures." That's what he was getting at when he said:

> Is there anything of which one can say, "Look! This is something new"? It was here already, long ago; it was here before our time (Eccles. 1:10).

Let's face it—the newness wears off. No matter what the relationship, experience, possession, or venture, we get used to it. All things have a tendency to get old, dusty, scratched, worn, rusty, wilted, moldy, even broken. When that happens we are left with one of three choices. We can find greater meaning and appreciation for that particular person, object, or task; or we can find a replacement; or we can drag along in limp frustration.

Take work, for example. Once I visited an automobile assembly plant. Each man had one job to do, and he was to perform it in exactly the same way on every car that passed down the assembly line. One guy had the fascinating task of screwing lug nuts onto truck wheels with an air gun. Twenty-four tedious times per truck he did his duty. Imagine that! Eight hours a day, five days a week, screwing nuts onto the wheels of trucks. Do you think he ever gets tired of his job? My guess is that the new wore off somewhere between the two-hundredth and three-hundredth lug nut.

Marriage also falls prey to tarnish. Young couples vibrate with affection and joyful friendship that first year or so. Then an unexpected wrinkle creases the relationship: they get used to each other. Sometimes they get bored. Their jobs are tedious, the bills absorb the money, lovemaking loses that brand-new feeling, and the four walls of home gradually start to close in. The survivors are the ones who polish a deeper shine into their partnership.

For many Christians, even their spiritual life has become moss-covered. They look upon prayer as a stale habit. Bible reading no longer enlivens them. Church worship and service are mechanically cranked out. It's Dullsville! Why? Good question, since God hasn't moved! Better yet, how? Too much shoreline living and not enough launching out into the deep, where the air refreshes, the spray dances, and the fish play in swirling currents.

Stagnation. It happens easily. Just get set in your ways and learn the creed of the drab by memory:

1. We are not ready for that yet.
2. We are doing fine just as we are (here in the mud).
3. It costs too much.
4. We've tried that before.
5. It's a nice idea, but it won't work.
6. Let someone else try it.
7. We've never done it that way.

Some people like things to stay in first gear, as if their motto were "Deadness is next to happiness." I'm not sure what causes such complacency, but isn't it a shame that once the new wears off some people are satisfied to let things run down and decay? Isn't it a sin to allow the true values of life to be leavened with the comfort of ritual?

You need to ask yourself, "How vital is it that I live with fervor, meaning, and fullness? Does it make a difference if I don't? Can it be done, anyway? And if it can, where do I begin?"

The Value of Routine

The hardest thing about life is that it's so daily—which means we need a strategy. Routine is just the ticket. Up to now you may have thought I had something against routine. Quite the contrary. But I am against "rut-tine." Is there a difference? To me there is.

"Rut-tine" is bland. It seeks and wants nothing more than mediocrity. It does not wish to challenge or be challenged; it neither dares to attempt nor attempts to dare. It does not dream; it only sleeps. "Rut-tine" is not stupid, just blissfully ignorant.

"Routine" is a horse of a different color in my understanding. Routine is steady and dependable, but flexible. It plans to finish something worthwhile every day, because trifles lead to triumph. It schedules carefully to avoid letting the sands of time slip through its fingers. Routine rides a mudder on life's track when the risk of bogging down is running high. When routine *does* get stuck, it patiently switches into four-wheel drive.

The Ecclesiastes preacher had it right—there is nothing new. But he failed to chart a course of correction for those frustrated by this principle. However, the whole of Scripture clears the fog—routine is a great place to start. Take a closer look.

Routine is necessary. Without it, very little gets accomplished. Much of boredom is caused by laziness and could be changed into fulfillment with a solid daily game plan. Even insects are smart enough to figure this out.

Go to the ant, you sluggard; consider its ways and be
wise! It has no commander, no overseer or ruler, yet it stores
its provisions in summer and gathers its food at harvest.
How long will you lie there, you sluggard? When will you
get up from your sleep? A little sleep, a little slumber, a little
folding of the hands to rest—and poverty will come on you
like a bandit and scarcity like an armed man (Prov. 6:6–11).

Not only is routine necessary to accomplish the natural
aspects of life, but it aids spiritual strength, too. Both David
and Daniel spoke of a regular prayer habit—morning, noon,
and night. And Jesus taught that cross carrying is a *daily*
task (Luke 9:23). It should be remembered, however, that
routine does not mean a certain thing has to be done exactly the same way every time. It simply means that essential things must be done with an unswerving consistency.
And always beneath the blue skies of freedom, instead of
the self-inflicted prison of monotony.

Routine must be flexible. Is it possible that we miss
some of life's riches by being closed to the subtle opportunities our rigid schedules disallow? Mark 2:1–12 tells of
Jesus' return to Capernaum. When the crowds heard that
he had come home, they swarmed the place. Packed to the
doorways and windowsills, the mob hushed to hear the
preaching of the Lord. About midway through the sermon a
strange occurrence took place. Up on the roof an opening
was made and a paralytic was let down on a mat with ropes.

Talk about interruptions! That blew the whole message.
Right? Not for Jesus. He saw the great faith of the man and
his friends. He broke routine. He stopped preaching and
concentrated all his attention upon the invalid. Moments
later the man arose, having been healed both physically and
spiritually.

If Jesus had been as inflexible as most of us, he would
probably have said, "Hey! What is this? Can't you see that
I'm busy? There's no room in here for you. You guys up
there on the roof, just raise him right out of here. And fix

the hole in the roof. Roofing isn't cheap these days, you know!"

We need to remain open to fresh ideas and new ways of doing things. We must be listening when opportunity knocks, because sometimes it only taps lightly. And if we are caught up in our tiny routine, we will miss God's immense schedule.

Routine must be broken sometimes. This is different from being "flexible." Flexibility bends, but there are times when routine must be deliberately broken. This can be anything from choosing an alternative route to work to taking an all-out vacation. One-minute daydreams during the long stretches of the day can help. Sixty seconds of mental escape are harmless. This is a wonderful time to meditate on Scripture, or to get a vision of your family's weekend outing, or to think on some other pure thought that refreshes you. This is sort of a mini-application of the Romans 12:2 concept of the "renewing of your mind." Try it and feel the frustration caused by tedium ebb out of you.

The Celebration of Life

Jesus said, "I am the resurrection and the life . . ." (John 11:25). Do you believe this? *The* life? Tall words, don't you think? That takes in every realm: physical, spiritual, and psychological; temporal and eternal. Which means we must have an intimate fellowship with The Life if we expect to have an energetic pulsebeat within our own.

We are created to be bored without Christ in our lives. In fact, that is one of the major themes of Ecclesiastes. Regardless of how much we try, no experience, person, or possession can satisfy our quest for a full life. And since we are prone to drift, we need to anchor ourselves to Christ.

In Christ we can really celebrate life. We can rejoice and praise God for the most plain circumstances. He turns the usual into the extraordinary through the power of his indwelling Spirit. Even nature takes on an enchantment unnoticed by eyes that see not. Who revels in the majesty of the Rockies more than the vital believer who recognizes the strength of God's arm in their craggy contours? Who lauds the splendors of spring more than the awakened soul who knows that new birth is more than just a season?

People who live with this kind of enthusiasm cannot contain it. They are compelled by their inner being to pour out their blessings on the confined prisoners of emptiness they meet. With a thrilling hope thumping inside, they are eager to heal the "paralyzed" in our day. Are you such a celebrant? Are you inviting other people to meet the Savior who takes boredom out of life and replaces it with purpose and passion? If not, no wonder you're having a hard time coping with "rut-tine." You are a light, and you are meant to shine with the sparkle of The Life! Jesus said so.

> You are the light of the world. A city on a hill cannot be hidden. Neither do people light a lamp and put it under a bowl. Instead they put it on its stand, and it gives light to everyone in the house. In the same way, let your light shine before men, that they may see your good deeds and praise your Father in heaven (Matt. 5:14–16).

Whenever I read these words I am reminded of the catching poetry of Edna St. Vincent Millay:

> My candle burns at both ends;
> It will not last the night;
> But, ah, my foes, and, oh, my friends—
> It gives a lovely light!

If you think tomorrow holds no possibilities for you, if you have given up on discovering an exhilarating realness in life, if you have grown accustomed to the ordinary, then you are missing out on authentic excitement.

Perhaps tomorrow at dawn there *will* be something new under the sun. You! Walking in the newness of life.

2

Who Says I'm Okay?

*Then I thought in my heart, "The fate of the fool will over-
take me also. What then do I gain by being wise?" I said in
my heart, "This too is meaningless"*   (Eccles. 2:15).

Several years ago we shuddered at the bold as-
sertiveness of the then-new self-awareness revolution.
Overnight, *I'm O.K., You're O.K.* became household chatter
and a national best-seller. Psychologists, educators, parents,
psychiatrists, counselors, and ministers have told us just
about all there is to know about developing a good self-
image. We've come a long way. And yet, in our personal
times of despairing frustration we secretly whisper, "Who
says I'm okay?"

Regardless of what we've been told about self-love, there
are days when we get fed up with ourselves. We try to be
self-aware; we give our best shot at being positive thinkers;
we reach down deep for a source of hidden confidence; we
even struggle for a balance of humility and self-esteem. But
we nonetheless get up-in-arms with ourselves. Though we
frequently grapple with our personal weaknesses in order
to forge improvements, we come up empty-handed. That's
frustrating!

Let me put it bluntly: no amount of "pep talk" is going to convince me that I'm always okay. I'm *not* always okay. Sometimes I'm downright rotten! I often fail to do the very things God directs me to do. At other times God gives me a red light, but I go straight ahead anyway, when I should be sitting still (Rom. 7:18–20). Sometimes I don't try to do my best when my best is desperately needed. Sometimes I get this terrible "I don't care" attitude. I particularly revel in self-pity. There is also a nasty nature within me that never wants to admit being in the wrong. And don't you sit there like nothing of this sort exists in you! Under the skin, we're all identical twins.

Defining Yourself

I can hear you now, "Thanks a lot, Earles! I just finished reading a Robert Schuller book on self-esteem. I was beginning to accept myself as part of God's marvelous creation, but now that you have just torn me to shreds I'm back to square one and thinking I'm no good. Thanks, I really needed that!"

Frustrated you, did I? Sorry, that was not my intention. I am merely trying to say that we all have down moments when self betrays us rather than portraying us as we really desire to be. We are by nature weak, not strong. We are prone to failure and incompleteness. Harping on the self-worth theme will not change that. Believing I am "somebody," for the wrong reasons, will only reduce me to nothing when I realize that I cannot live up to my self-expectations by myself.

"So we're all a bunch of nobodies?" you cry. Not exactly. But apart from Christ we depreciate our productivity to zero. A tree that will not bear fruit is a very maddening thing. So we often get mad at ourselves, because we remain unfruitful, caught up in the worth of ourselves rather than the worth of our Lord. Yet Jesus told us:

". . . . No branch can bear fruit by itself; it must remain
in the vine. Neither can you bear fruit unless you remain in
me. I am the vine; you are the branches. If a man remains
in me and I in him, he will bear much fruit; apart from me
you can do nothing" (John 15:4–5).

Pungent words. Words, I might add, that ought to be the
bull's-eye of any self-awareness therapy. We are bound to
give up on ourselves if we make no progress, since we corre-
late competence and achievement with feelings of worth.
Yet our fruitbearing is absolutely related to our attachment
to Christ.

"So we're nobodies if we don't produce?" you wonder.
No, that is definitely a wrong conclusion. Unfortunately,
many workaholics live by such a creed. They think they
must drive themselves to an early grave by outdoing yesterday's accomplishments. The workaholic grows weary with
himself unless he can achieve the pinnacle of "success" and
then some.

Actually, the true worth of an individual has very little to
do with performance. One's real value is rooted in love, not
labor. I do not have to *try* to be somebody; I *am* somebody
because God made me and he loves me. As Martin Luther
said, "God does not love us because we are valuable; we are
valuable because God loves us." This truth is the clear
message of Scripture:

Whoever is wise, let him heed these things and consider
the great love of the LORD (Ps. 107:43).

For great is his love toward us, and the faithfulness of the
LORD endures forever (Ps. 117:2).

And so we know and rely on the love God has for us . . .
(1 John 4:16).

So, then, you are somebody because God loves you. And
you can rely on his love! However, to help you feel personal
worth, Christ enters into a vine/branches relationship with

you when you abide in him. The result is, you bring forth fruit—the best "you" comes alive! Apart from this loving, living fellowship with Christ, you are bound to be frustrated and feel like a nobody.

Dividing Yourself

Most of us live a divided existence, a subtle brand of schizophrenia. On the outside we project one person, while on the inside we conceal a second identity. The outside person is the one everybody knows us to be; the inside person is the one only *we* know. Why do we cut ourselves in two? Why do we hide our real self? Why do we find it so difficult to relax and be natural?

Often it is because we are frustrated and dissatisfied with that inner self and fear that acting normal will bring rejection. We reason, "If I don't like myself, then nobody else will either." So we try to look better than what we think we are. As one person put it, "I'm afraid to be who I really am, because if I do you might hate me, and I'm all I've got!"

In quiet desperation we settle for a self-constructed schizoid personality. Privacy protects us—from everyone but ourselves. We would do almost anything to avoid the pain of being rejected by others, but we rough-arm ourselves and play mental videotapes that force the real self into a surer seclusion.

And what kind of pre-recorded video cassettes do we allow to replay over and over again in our minds? Painful ones—bitter reminders that prove us worthless and further frustrate us:

1. *Impossible standards.* If we set expectations for ourselves that we couldn't possibly live up to, we will govern ourselves with a rigid "interiority" complex and keep a constant surveillance on our behavior to catch any tiny mistake. Such paragons of excellence overdemand of themselves and end up heaping on self-blame for every failure. Perfectionists usually let their strict regimen filter into

their spiritual life. Their carefully crafted, pharisaical regulations are supposed to be a fast ticket to godliness. But, as always happens with legalism, they only exchange one ball and chain for another.

"It is for freedom that Christ has set us free. Stand firm, then, and do not let yourselves be burdened again by a yoke of slavery" (Gal. 5:1). Christ has made us free, but some people won't permit themselves to enjoy that freedom. Not only is his freedom a freedom from sin, but it is also a freedom to fulfill God's design of Christ in you—the best person you can be. The Christlike you!

Although Christ sets us free from an unachievable ideal, he empowers us to become an unlimited instrument, living a life that is real. He does not, however, give us permission to run wild. Paul explained this candidly to the Galatians who were frustrating their faith with impossible standards: "You, my brothers, were called to be free. But do not use your freedom to indulge the sinful nature . . ." (Gal. 5:13).

And Peter had these words of warning for Christians scattered apart because of persecution and thus susceptible to old legalism: "Live as free men, but do not use your freedom as a cover-up for evil; live as servants of God" (1 Peter 2:16).

Free yourself. Promise not to intimidate the imperfect you anymore with severe interior inspections by which you are certain to fail the white-glove test. But don't trash the periodic self-examinations that help to keep you spiritually fit.

2. *Physical flaws.* Never has there been a time when fashion, facials, and fitness meant so much to people. To a degree that isn't bad. But society has now so overemphasized body dynamics that anyone less than glamorous by prevailing standards is apt to feel self-conscious. Of course, changing some undesirable features—such as overweight, an unflattering hairstyle, or dental problems— might help you feel more comfortable with yourself and make it easier for you to reveal the genuine you.

We all must learn, however, that we have physical and mental limitations that are God-given. Being limited in a certain area forces us to develop the areas in which we are more talented and naturally endowed. Whether our abilities relate to intelligence or physical aptitude, we should never give in to self-pressure to measure up to the world's idea of beauty and rank, for "[God] knows how we are formed, he remembers that we are dust" (Ps. 103:14).

Are those not tremendous words? God knows our very limitations and our physical flaws, and he loves us anyway. Our frailty is no secret to him, though we may hide it well from others. How wonderful that we don't have to arrive at "status" to please him!

3. *Past humiliation.* Many people torture themselves with the hurts of the past, possibly remembering as far back as childhood. Although salvation in Christ is the beginning of re-creating our lives, and it *is* a cleansing transformation, it does not erase our memories. Whether those mental souvenirs are pleasant or unpleasant, they remain filed away, able to bring private moments of either cheer or frustration.

In his book *Putting Away Childish Things*, David Seamands pinpoints this so well, "The memories that seem to grip and grind us, that have an almost hypnotic sway and power over us, are memories of deep emotional pain, resentment, hate, fear, or embarrassment. Sometimes it is a terrible mixture of all these."

Paul shared with the Philippians his personal therapy tactics for past humiliations when he said, ". . . .Forgetting what is behind and straining toward what is ahead, I press on toward the goal to win the prize for which God has called me heavenward in Christ Jesus" (Phil. 3:13–14). "Forget?" you ask. "But how do you propose that I forget something that is lodged in my memory? I can't just pretend that it isn't registered up there."

I agree. Surprised? Don't be. This isn't more theoretical stuff; it's practical. "Forget" is the Greek word *epilanthanomai.* That's a mouthful! But it's also insightful. It means "to neglect to remember." In other words, when unpleasant memories crop up, we should prayerfully hand them over to the Lord, and then we should refuse to let ourselves dwell on them.

4. *Suppressed guilt.* Here I'm not talking about the self-spun, false guilt of perfectionism, but about true guilt, the kind that relates to sinful behavior and/or thoughts. When guilt over sin goes unconfessed and is suppressed, it nags at a person, draining energy and optimism. Guilt is a potent frustrater. But the words of Proverbs 28:13 still hold true: "He who conceals his sins does not prosper, but whoever confesses and renounces them finds mercy."

5. *Character weaknesses.* Wouldn't it be nice if you could be a mighty fortress safe from the attacks of Satan? What if you had no spiritual soft spots? What if you had the power to respond to every situation perfectly, in full control?

Hebrews 12:1 implies a greater reality: "Therefore, since we are surrounded by such a great cloud of witnesses, let us throw off everything that hinders and the sin that so easily entangles, and let us run with perseverance the race marked out for us." Did you notice that phrase "the sin that so easily entangles"? What sin is that? With each of us it is different, relating to our individual character weaknesses. What sins are you most prone to commit?

A discouraged woman, exasperated by her spiritual defeats, once told me "Brent, sometimes I hate myself for being so weak. I give what I think is my best effort, but it isn't enough. Before long I lapse back. I'm just so weak, and I can hardly stand to live with myself because of it!" I think the personal association each of us finds with those words is closer than we would like to admit.

I replied, "Where do I go to join the club? The truth is, we're all weak. Even though we don't want to believe it. We want to believe that we have the strength to win over anything. But we don't—at least, not in ourselves! Our feeble spots, as well as our strong ones, need the protection of

God's armor. Most of all we need to abandon ourselves to the vivacious, Herculean power of the Holy Spirit."

Denying One's Self

Since the day I yielded myself to the lordship of Christ, two of his sayings have provided me with spiritual gravity. They have literally held me in place:

> Then he said to them all: "If anyone would come after me, he must deny himself and take up his cross daily and follow me" (Luke 9:23).
> Jesus replied, "No one who puts his hand to the plow and looks back is fit for service in the kingdom of God" (Luke 9:62).

Too many times my self has wanted to look back. My vain self begs to be touched by me, stroked for reassurance. But the fruitful Spirit has proven himself a better Master. He does not leave me unguarded or unguided. I can trust him when I cannot trust myself.

Denying self, though, is not weird, ascetic punishment. Some people think that humble dependence on Christ necessitates self-rejection. Wrong! Self-denial does not equal self-rejection. In self-denial, self dies daily (Gal. 2:20) to allow the Holy Spirit's full strength to be released; but in self-rejection, self remains alive to be tormented and put down. The Spirit is thus unable to complete the image of God in us.

Colossians 3:2–3 contains an interesting admonition: "Set your minds on things above, not on earthly things. For you died, and your life is now hidden with Christ in God." Did you hear that? When you accepted Christ, you died! Your old self was nailed with Christ to the cross, and when he came out of the tomb, it was so that your old self could never frustrate you again.

That makes you better than okay!

3

Another Peter Principle

Patience is better than pride. Do not be quickly provoked in your spirit, for anger resides in the lap of fools (Eccles. 7:8b–9).

D<small>r.</small> Lawrence J. Peter and Raymond Hall caused heads to nod in agreement when they came out with their best-seller, *The Peter Principle,* a book about business and management. Judging by the tenor of their writing, it appears that Peter and Hall penned their precepts out of irritation with what they saw to be a lazy business world. In essence *The Peter Principle* says, "In a hierarchy, every employee tends to rise to his level of incompetence. . . . Work is accomplished by employees who have not yet reached their level of incompetence." Sounds like the authors were irritated cynics, doesn't it?

"Irritation" is another way to spell frustration. Whether it consists of the neighbor's dog digging graves in your vegetable garden or an all-out confrontation with the lousy driver ahead of you, irritation can wrinkle your day. How true that the "incompetence" of some thing or some person can push us from being irritable into being downright irrational!

I mentioned driving, so let me use it to illustrate my point. Here's the scenario: Mr. Sunday Driver is directing a sightseeing tour on the freeway for a carload of passengers and doesn't realize that he has been running abreast of a senior-citizen transport bus for the last three miles. In the passing lane behind Mr. Sunday Driver is Mr. Indy 500. He's in a hurry and is slowly becoming Mr. Hot-Under-the-Collar. The motorcade continues to creep along at a pace intolerable to Mr. Indy 500, so he starts flashing his lights. When nothing changes, he bears down on his horn. Still no response. Desperately wanting to get around these "jokers," Indy beats on his steering wheel and starts screaming. Why he is *screaming* I'm not sure, since apparently neither of the irritants is able to hear his horn.

Indy considers using a creative-driving method—passing on the shoulder. Just as he steers onto the grass divider, his left front wheel drops off the edge into a muddy rut, throwing his car into convulsions. Miraculously, he avoids an accident. Now he is berserk! Racing to catch up with the convoy, he rides Mr. S.D.'s bumper. He has decided to "teach him a lesson."

When S.D. finally pulls over, Indy is nearly psychotic. He pulls alongside the slowpoke and begins lecturing him with finger pointing and vocabulary words found only in slang dictionaries. S.D. and his passengers are quite amused, which incites Indy to *really* teach them a lesson! He zooms by and slashes over in front of them, slamming on his brakes. S.D. has to jam on his brakes, which irritates him and all his passengers. So he pulls out in the passing lane again, but Indy cuts over in front of him. To further educate Mr. Sunday Driver, Indy slows to a creep, as cars zip past them on the right. S.D. hasn't the slightest idea why this kook is terrorizing him. At the same time, Indy is confident that the lesson is well-learned, so he speeds off, declaring himself to be the last sane driver in the world. Note that he is now much nearer a bleeding ulcer than before. In his state of mind, it will take him 6.2 hours to recuperate!

Why have you pulled a sheet over your head? Does this sound embarrassingly familiar? Maybe the highway poses no problem for your temper, but bring on an unbalanced washing machine and your hair stands on end. In fact, the list of irritations is infinite:

hot weather	long-winded preachers
cold weather	cats who miss the box
windy weather	$.10 raises
rainy weather	soap in your eyes
two-year-olds	dogs who bark at bedtime
teenagers	"Dynasty"
flat tires	people who watch "Dynasty"
speed traps	phone solicitors
waiting	slow restaurants
utility-rate increases	leftovers
news reporters	bills
taxes	doctors
telethons	high interest rates
surprise visitors	diets
junk mail	vitamin advocates
ironing	muddy shoes
bagworms	people
anything broken	rock music
gossips	weeds
power outages	spills
pushy salespeople	being late
making ends meet	cigarette smoke

The irritating thing about irritations is that they come in bundles. For some reason they never come singly, or even in two's. No, all forty days' and forty nights' worth come flooding down at once. Or so it seems. But then it's hard to be even-minded at these times. One solid irritation absorbed in a heavy dose is enough to start a chain reaction. Suddenly, everything becomes maddening. Nod if you've been there before.

Permit me to introduce you to a fellow in Scripture who knew about this source of frustration. His name is Peter. This unique disciple provides us with a practical illustration of dealing with irritability. His "Peter principle" probably went something like this: "In a lifetime, every day tends to rise to its level of frustration." But the longer he walked with Jesus, the more he learned that this wasn't true. Grab your Bible and let's have a look.

The First Incident

Let's pick up with Matthew 16:20, where Peter had just exclaimed the startling revelation given to him from heaven, that Jesus is the Christ, the Son of the living God. After that, Jesus began to explain to his disciples that he would eventually go to Jerusalem and be crucified. The more Peter heard of this, the more aggravated he became. Finally, when he couldn't take another word, he shouted, "Never, Lord! This shall never happen to you!" (v. 22).

The impetuous disciple could not imagine life without his beloved Master. It irritated him that the bliss he was enjoying might be snuffed out by a sudden interruption of plans. Furthermore, why did Jesus have to ruin such a fun day by bringing up something as ugly as a crucifixion?

Jesus had an unusual answer, "Out of my sight, Satan!" (v. 23). Why did he say that? Why didn't he say something like, "Peter, don't be foolish" or "Shame on you for thinking I could be wrong about anything"? Why did he call Peter "Satan"?

In a moment of weakness, Peter had become the devil's mouthpiece. So Jesus was actually addressing Satan, whose invisible presence was very real. No doubt Peter was astounded and ashamed that he had allowed his personal irritation to become such a folly of words.

Like Peter, all of us have permitted unexpected interruptions to crush us. To be sure, Christ's death was more than a mere kink in the hope-filled future. But Peter overlooked a vital promise: Jesus said he would be resurrected to life on the third day (v. 21). Similarly, we can anticipate a purpose behind God's design of "irritating" our pocket-planners.

The Second Incident

Now take a look at Matthew 18:21, where Peter asked, "Lord, how many times shall I forgive my brother when he sins against me? Up to seven times?" In essence he wanted to know how long he had to put up with a person who was more than the average human could bear. What do you think? When does a person reach the point-of-no-forgiveness? How long must we allow someone to antagonize, abuse, manipulate, push, and take advantage of us?

Jesus stayed in character. He gave another dynamic answer, "I tell you, not seven times, but seventy-seven times" (v. 22). I wonder if Jesus' answers ever got on Peter's nerves? I mean, Jesus never answered a single question the way Peter expected, just as we are often amazed that God does not reply as we would wish. His principles are greater than our penchants.

Peter was in need of another principle. Jesus supplied him with a perfect one: patient forgiveness is what we owe our irritants, because it is that very kind of forbearance that the Father shows us.

The Third Incident

John's Gospel records a curious episode. After an evening meal, Jesus began to wash and dry the disciples' feet. When Peter's turn came, he offered another in his series of incredulous questions, "Lord, are you going to wash my feet?" (John 13:6). Jesus assured him that there was a reason behind the footwashing and that he would understand it later—to which Peter replied, "No, you shall never wash my feet" (v. 8).

What would you guess the Lord said to that? Something like: "Fine! If you want dirty feet, have them"? No. Matter-of-factly, he commented, "Unless I wash you, you have no part with me." That provokes an interesting question: is footwashing mandatory for becoming a disciple of Christ? Not at all. So then, what did Jesus mean? Glance down to verses 15–16:

> "I have set you an example that you should do as I have done for you. I tell you the truth, no servant is greater than his master, nor is a messenger greater than the one who sent him."

Jesus feared that his disciples would forget that they were *servants.* By washing their feet and commanding them to be equally humble toward one another, he was diminishing the possibility that they would exasperate each other after he left. If Peter had denied the Lord the privilege of serving him, later he would lack the humility of spirit needed to serve others. Those governed by a servant's heart are not too easily agitated. Peter needed that.

This "Peter principle" is also right down our alley. Many of the frustrations we experience through irritation come because we are self-centered and do not have the mind of a servant. If our main interest is being served, rather than serving, we are bound to grow impatient when things do not go our way. That's exactly what the Ecclesiastes preacher was emphasizing when he said that "patience is better than pride. Do not be quickly provoked in your spirit, for anger resides in the lap of fools" (Eccles. 7:8b–9).

The Fourth Incident

Near the end of his earthly ministry, Jesus told his disciples, "You will all fall away, for it is written: 'I will strike the shepherd, and the sheep will be scattered.' But after I have risen, I will go ahead of you into Galilee" (Mark 14:27–28).

Peter once again grew irritated with such unpleasant news and fired back, "Even if all fall away, I will not" (v. 29). I applaud his loyalty. And, frankly, I can identify with him. That sounds like something I would have said. Likewise, the Lord's response would have pierced me just as I'm sure it did Peter.

Jesus answered, "I tell you the truth, today—yes, to-night—before the rooster crows twice you yourself will dis-own me three times" (v. 30). Was Jesus merely prophesying about Peter, or was he also revealing something deeper about Peter's very bent toward impulsiveness when faced with difficulty?

> But Peter insisted emphatically, "Even if I have to die with you, I will never disown you." And all the others said the same (Mark 14:31).

Of course, we know better, don't we? He did deny Jesus. Peter did the most awful, reprehensible thing at our Lord's hour of betrayal. But he represented us and acted the very way we would have, if we had been there.

The Fifth Incident

After Christ's resurrection, it was time for the disciples to pick up with the vibrant message of the gospel. But they were slow starters. So Jesus arranged a clambake beside the Sea of Tiberias (John 21). There he rallied them by showing how fruitful they would be in fishing for *souls*—he guided them in the miraculous catch of fish.

When they had eaten, Jesus turned his attention toward Peter, still chiseling the rough edges off his rash follower. The time was soon to come when impatience could cost Peter the effectiveness that would be needed to lead the others. The Lord was giving him the last installment of his personal treatment. They walked, just the two of them, along the seashore.

As they walked, Peter turned and saw John following them. Peter was irritated that the Lord required so much of him but never seemed to push John and the others as hard. He pointed at John and griped, "Lord, what about him?" (John 21:21).

Jesus answered with a thoughtful rebuke—a good technique to use on those who frequently succumb to petty irritations. His words are classic: "If I want him to remain alive until I return, what is that to you? You must follow me" (v. 22). In other words, "Why are you upsetting yourself with business that doesn't concern you? Concentrate on yourself." For most of us, it is no small chore to keep ourselves on track, much less someone else.

How many times have we reacted like Peter did? Something doesn't go our way, and so we lash out in frustration, wondering why "that guy over there" has it so easy. We only frustrate ourselves further by getting irritated at the thought that no one else is being cumbered like we are.

Incidentally, what did become of John? It's so fitting that I can barely refrain a laugh whenever I think on it. John became Peter's preaching companion. The fellow who Peter worried wouldn't have similar responsibility turned out to be his very intimate sidekick.

Peter's New Principle

Peter matured and helped shape history by boldly preaching the gospel in the days of the early church. And though he always maintained that characteristic excitable spirit, he came to have fewer lapses of irritability. Rarely was he defeated by frustration. Peter became so even-tempered that he later wrote these appropriate words:

> The end of all things is near. Therefore be clear minded and self-controlled so that you can pray. . . . Each one should

use whatever gift he has received to serve others, faithfully administering God's grace in its various forms. If anyone speaks, he should do it as one speaking the very words of God. If anyone serves, he should do it with the strength God provides, so that in all things God may be praised through Jesus Christ . . . (1 Peter 4:7, 10–11).

Make note of the key words and ideas he used to signify the patient believer:

clear minded	careful with words
self-controlled	spiritual strength
humble serving	calm spirit

If Peter's former principle had been: "In a lifetime, every day tends to rise to its level of frustration," then his new principle must have become: "Through Christ, any servant can rise to a higher level of tranquility."

Go—and let your irritations control you no more.

4

The Proverbial
Personality Conflict

*Do not pay attention to every word people say, or you may
hear your servant cursing you—for you know in your heart
that many times you yourself have cursed others* (Eccles.
7:21–22).

I love *Peanuts*, that crazy gang of cartoon kids
created by Charles Schulz. Their way of expressing true-to-
life situations has made these characters household names
and favorites with children and adults alike. One of Lucy's
gripe sessions stands out in my memory. She was complaining to Charlie Brown in her typical fussy style. Evidently
not everything was going her way, and frustration had
tripped her aggravation button. With calm hostility, poor
Lucy shrugged her shoulders and said, "Actually, I love
mankind." Charlie listened, his face expressionless. Then
she raised her hands in total disgust, "It's people I can't
stand!"

Lucy speaks perfectly for us. We really love our fellow-
men, and most of the time we get along fine with them. It's
just those few individuals who drive us batty that make us
grumble under our breath, "Argh! I can't stand that per-

son!" Ever feel that way or say that about anybody? Yeah, me too.

When Will Rogers, the famous laid-back humorist, said he never met a man he didn't like, it must have been because he never met some of the people the rest of us know. Problem people and people problems are a Grade A source of frustration. Try as we may, we just can't help it: there are some people we simply can't "click" with. Like the north poles of two magnets, we can be forced together but never made to stick. Because of personality differences, we're prone to have conflicts with others.

Sure, Scripture has a lot to say about interpersonal relationships. Try some of these on for size:

> Live in harmony with one another . . . (Rom. 12:16).
>
> Be completely humble and gentle; be patient, bearing with one another in love. Make every effort to keep the unity of the Spirit through the bond of peace (Eph. 4:2–3).
>
> If you have any encouragement from being united with Christ, if any comfort from his love, if any fellowship with the Spirit, if any tenderness and compassion, then make my joy complete by being like-minded, having the same love, being one in spirit and purpose (Phil. 2:1–2).
>
> Bear with each other and forgive whatever grievances you may have against one another . . . (Col. 3:13).
>
> Do not repay evil with evil or insult with insult, but with blessing, because to this you were called so that you may inherit a blessing (1 Peter 3:9).
>
> Dear friends, let us love one another, for love comes from God. Everyone who loves has been born of God and knows God. Whoever does not love does not know God, because God is love (1 John 4:7–8).

"Enough!" you say? I know what you mean. Rereading those verses makes me want to crawl under a rug to hide my embarrassment and shame. Too many times I have welcomed the vindictive voices of my pride that whisper to me, "You don't have to put up with that. You're a published author and pastor of a metropolitan church." Of which the

Holy Spirit must think, "Next thing you know, he'll be after my position in the Trinity." Can you relate?

Personality conflicts usually come because pride has gotten in the way. What happens is that we play comparison games and imagine ourselves to be in combative competition with someone who has a different slant on things than we do. We fear losing. Of course, there's really nothing at stake except the satisfaction we can feel from being one-up on the other guy.

The real cause of a competitive spirit within relationships is a lack of self-esteem. It's one thing to give everything we have to overcome a problem or reach a specific goal; it's quite another thing to expend energies intended for achievement on the pitiless task of winning over others. Whenever "beating" somebody becomes essential to our self-appreciation, we have already missed the opportunity for a much greater reward—serving.

Not all people compete against those with whom they have conflicts. Instead of taking the my-way-is-the-only-way approach, some people adopt a who-needs-you? attitude and simply walk away. They choose for other people to lose, too. By "writing off" irregular people, we save ourselves the trouble of ever having to evaluate our own personality weaknesses that contribute to bad relationships.

That doesn't mean a person has to play Pendulum Roulette and swing to the other extreme—"Let me be your doormat." Permitting pushier personalities to command the upper hand by following their demands buries your own individuality. When this happens, nice guys may not finish last, but they do get awfully frustrated. Always submitting during personality clashes eventually boomerangs into "I can't take any more of this." Early on in the conflict a firecracker of a comment would have made a point. Now, because of bottled disagreements, a long-delayed confrontation is more likely to produce atom-bomb results.

"Conflict" is a scary word. The very thought of it sends chills of tension through the back of your neck. Who needs it? While I'm sure you agree with my sentiments, we must admit that, like it or not, if Christians are going to build strong fellowship ties and extend themselves in witnessing and discipling through the teamwork effort of their local churches, personalities are occasionally going to go bump in the night.

Realizing that some disagreements are unavoidable, it may do us some good to remember David Augsburger's words about conflict in his book *Caring Enough to Confront:*

> Conflict is natural, normal, neutral, and sometimes even delightful. It can turn into painful or disastrous ends, but it doesn't need to. Conflict is neither good nor bad, right nor wrong. Conflict simply is. How we view, approach and work through our differences does—to a large extent—determine our whole life pattern.

To be sure, whenever a personality conflict persists but is suppressed, overcharged irritation is fed by feelings of helplessness and hopelessness. The parties involved soon grow sick of each other and are likely to become dirty in their interpersonal dealings. This intensifies the struggle until the relationship finally disintegrates into a cold war, and bitterness begins to wrap its thorny vines around its victims.

Accepting Differences

Tolerance. That's a big part of minimizing conflicts. Jonathan Swift, the satirical writer of *Gulliver's Travels,* said, "We have just enough religion to make us hate, but not enough to make us love one another." Looks like he'd been around the block a few times. The way brothers and sisters slap and fuss and feud goes on in God's family, too. It's an ugly truth to admit, but some of the meanest, most intolerant characters in town are supposed to be Christians.

These lines of anonymous sarcasm may secretly be their motto:

> Believe as I believe—no more, no less;
> That I am right (and no one else) confess.
> Feel as I feel, think only as I think;
> Eat what I eat, and drink but what I drink.
> Look as I look, do always as I do;
> And then—and only then—I'll fellowship with you.

However, Christians should go beyond tolerance in their relationships. Just as important as forbearing glaring dissimilarities is learning to appreciate the qualities that make each fellow believer unique. Remember, God believes in individualism. Although he tells us to have unity, he doesn't call for uniformity. God didn't create us to be identical clones; he made originals only. A good many conflicts between Christians occur because they are bent on changing each other. This is the way of the "I'm right" gang. By disavowing a disapproving attitude, we can begin to climb the peak of interpersonal peace.

The apostle Paul evidently suspected that some of the people in the church at Rome were having a tough time accepting each other. He wrote some sharp instructions to people who, because of their conflicting opinions and petty disagreements, were nit-picking back and forth until their testimonies and sanity were lost. Paul's pointers for positive relationships are right on target:

1. *We belong to the Lord.* "If we live, we live to the Lord; and if we die, we die to the Lord. So, whether we live or die, we belong to the Lord" (Rom. 14:8). Before we reject a fellow believer over something as insignificant as our opposite personalities, it might do us some good to remember how God feels about that person. Ask yourself, "Isn't God quite capable of sanding off someone else's rough edges without using me as the sandpaper?" You see, God is committed to refining his children, and he knows which of their weaknesses need attention better than we do.

2. *We account to the Lord.* We know intellectually that it's wrong to pass condemning judgment on others. Yet, when we expect people to meet our criteria for being accepted (and spurn them when they don't), that's exactly what we end up doing. In essence, we give the impression that those who don't come up to "spec" on our personality meter are accountable to us for their inexcusable selves. Paul said otherwise, "You, then, why do you judge your brother? Or why do you look down on your brother? For we will all stand before God's judgment seat" (Rom. 14:10). People don't have to answer to us; but all of us will answer to God. Aren't you more concerned about the answer God requires of you than whether or not God is going to remember to straighten out the other guy? Perhaps we should consider the cartoon that depicts a beautiful sunset and has the question written across the skies, "Are you trying to take the job of your boss?"

3. *We are accepted by the Lord.* As unlikable as some people may be, if God accepts them so should we. Listen to Romans 15:7: "Accept one another, then, just as Christ accepted you, in order to bring praise to God." It brings no praise to God when we allow barriers to drive us apart—especially when the barrier amounts to nothing more than a difference in our chemistry. Obviously, we can't be best friends with everybody, but that hardly gives us the freedom to pronounce anathemas on people who irritate us. The humble servant accepts others even if they don't return the favor.

Not to overstate the issue, but we are pros at sizing up people—categorizing them, predicting their actions, and sticking them into a pigeonhole that fits our prescribed stereotype. I recall how this was done to Ann (not her real name), a lovely young woman who had the unpleasant trait of talking too loudly and, as a result, came off to others as a brash, bossy person. In a lot of ways she was her own worst enemy. Although she was outgoing and loved to be around groups of people, Ann's annoying behavior pattern caused her to be painfully rejected. Being beautiful didn't help matters. The young women in Ann's church perceived her as a threat because of her high energy level and stunning attractiveness. On the outside it looked as if Ann was confident and self-assured, but inwardly she was fearful and insecure.

One Sunday evening, after a long week of enduring cruel statements and agonizing put-downs, Ann attempted to kill herself. When she counseled with me later, she said, "You're probably wondering why I did this." I told her that "why" was important, but that "what you are going to do about it" was the real issue. Desperate to rid herself of the frustration of why she wanted to die, Ann fought through tears: "I don't want to live if I've got to keep facing constant rejection. It's unfair!"

Ann's right. Since Christians are already rejected by the world, what will become of them if they are not accepted by their fellow believers? To what extent can we allow personality conflicts to drive us apart? Can we tolerate the exclusivity of cliques in our churches, which increases the risk that some believers will feel like they don't fit in? Is this really what Jesus had in mind when he taught his disciples how to fellowship? The absence of satisfying interpersonal relationships is a serious frustration for many Christians. They are made to feel like outsiders, and that's unfair, no matter how you slice it.

Listening Carefully

Dale Carnegie has become a household name because of his little best-seller *How to Win Friends and Influence People*. He writes:

> If you want to know how to make people shun you and laugh at you behind your back and even despise you, here is the recipe: Never listen to anyone for long. Talk incessantly about yourself. If you have an idea while the other fellow is talking, don't wait for him to finish. He isn't as smart as

you. Why waste your time listening to his idle chatter? Bust
right in and interrupt him in the middle of a sentence.

Solomon said something similar in his wise way: "He
who answers before listening—that is his folly and his
shame" (Prov. 18:13). Have you ever caught yourself at this?
Do you play "I Can Beat That" games? That's the ego cha-
rade we act out whenever we wish others would hurry up
with telling the event from their day or idea from their
thoughts, because we can't wait to top their tidbit with a
clever article of our own. This form of one-upmanship in-
directly communicates that we think *we* are smarter and
therefore deserve to be heard more than the other guy.

Especially insensitive people even use this technique on
close business associates, Christian friends, and family
members. Since they obviously love the sound of their own
voices, why would they bother listening to someone else's?
We wonder how we can get their attention. Usually these
types do not really listen to the person who's talking anyway, so what good does it do to approach them?

This disease, "waxius eardrumitis," eventually causes
misunderstandings and sometimes outright anger. It reminds me of a quote that was directed by an incensed al-
most-conversationalist to an interrupting, misjudging
chum: "I know you believe you understand what you think
I said, but I am not sure you realize that what you heard is
not what I said."

Few things in life are more gratifying than being listened
to and knowing that our words are being accepted as funny
or pertinent or thoughtful. One of the great causes of interpersonal conflicts is that two talkers get together and neither knows how to listen, or two listeners get together and
neither knows what to say. The solution is not always as
simplistic as having one talker and one listener. Rather, we
all must learn the vital importance of being "participating
listeners." The good listener will participate in a conversation without getting into a foolish debate. Since he

realizes that understanding wins more people than arguments, he demonstrates Christian love by caring enough to really hear what the other person is trying to say. Even if he strongly disagrees with it.

Remember Ann? Being a participating listener could have eased her agony.

Perhaps we should take still another lesson from Jesus. For he who said, "He who has ears, let him hear" (Matt. 13:43), practiced what he preached. He listened.

Communicating Well

The Proverbs verse is not referring to most of us when it succinctly describes ideal communication: "A word aptly spoken is like apples of gold in settings of silver" (Prov. 25:11). Have you ever met a person who always knows the right thing to say at the right time? Wouldn't it be wonderful to have such glorious communication skills as to never misspeak in any situation? To be able to communicate freely with every sort of person—friend or enemy—and flow with the most timely, well-chosen words? Sorry, but that's not going to happen in the real world.

Naturally, being the imperfect beings that we are, we don't always use "lovable" language. Often, when upset, we say things that we don't really mean and take out our frustrations on innocent people. In the heat of conflict we are tempted to use any tactic that will help us get the upper hand. Raised voices and red faces are not strangers to situations in which we feel that we've gotten a raw deal. "Strike back!" is our instinctive, red-alert reaction. We hate to lose. And yet, in personality battles, does anybody win?

Aesop's fable about the wind and the sun is for those who foolishly engage in personality combat. The wind and the sun argued over which was the stronger. The wind decided to make a contest of it and said, "Do you see that man down there? I can make him take his coat off quicker than you can." The sun stepped behind the clouds while the wind raged and howled and blew, but the old man just bundled up all the more.

The wind finally wore himself out and settled down to give the sun his chance. Soon the warm, bright sun had the old man smiling and relaxed. He wiped his brow, pulled off his coat, and went merrily upon his way. The sun won because it knew that "nothing is so strong as gentleness, and nothing is so gentle as true strength."

In the communication process, gentleness may be the single most effective weapon against offensive attacks. It enables us to view the positive side of other people and to avoid feeling as if we have something to lose or a point to prove. We are free to be ourselves and to accept others as they are. Ann needed that. So does Lucy.

5

Home-Maid Insanity

"Meaningless! Meaningless!" says the Teacher. "Utterly meaningless! Everything is meaningless" (Eccles. 1:2).

As Jane and I made an unusually quiet trip home after the Sunday-evening church services recently, I could tell that her mind was going ninety miles per minute. Having grown tense because of the silence, and curious to know what she was thinking, I asked the commonly used question "What's wrong?" to get inside her world.

"I don't want to go home," she said abruptly and in one of those depressive tones that really means, "Something else is bothering me, but you will have to ask me more to find out what it is. And if you don't, I'm going to be mad at you."

I paused for a second, trying to be as lighthearted as possible, and said, "Aw, honey, it's been such a hectic week—and next week's going to be busy, too—why don't you want to go home? We need to sit back and relax and catch our breath."

Then she started mumbling. A deep frown was creased into her brow. I knew Jane was working up to some dramatic statement, because she kept tilting her head from one shoulder to the other. At the same time she was gesturing with her hands, as if they knew what she wanted to say but couldn't put the words into her mouth. Suddenly the words popped out: "I need your help next Thursday to clean the house."

It hit me why she didn't want to go home, but before I could say anything, she was no longer at a loss for words: "Have you seen the house this week?" She wasn't really looking for an answer but only needed to blow off some steam. "It's a mess, an absolute disaster!" Her gestures became a little exaggerated—a sure sign of frustration. "I've been so busy this week that I haven't had time to clean anything. I'm behind on everything! Have you seen the kitchen! It's full of dishes and trash. We've only been home long enough to sleep. Have you seen the bathroom? I haven't even finished last week's laundry and it's already next week. Have you seen the carpet? When am I going to catch up on my ironing, I haven't even vacuumed! Just look at everything when you walk in the front door—just look at it! Do you think I want to look at it? I don't. I don't even want to see it. If I see it, I have to think about how much work I have to do. And I don't have time to do it until next Thursday. I can't stand being this far behind. I'm going crazy. Do you hear me? I'm going crazy!"

"Sure, I can help you on Thursday," I answered very nonchalantly.

Jane relaxed and took a deep breath. Both of us were surprised at my willingness to clean house. Although I've been liberated from many of my male-chauvinist ideas, I'm still fighting the primal urgings from within that tell me that domestic work is a woman's responsibility. It used to be universally accepted that the woman took care of the inside domain and men kept up the garage and lawn. Not anymore. In our fast-paced, two-income-household society, dust rags and dishwashers are no longer foreign to the male gender (yours truly included).

Some weary wife is going to read these words and then beg her husband to read them, too. Naturally, his reaction to my domestication will be that I have been beaten by the N.O.W. and cannot be trusted. "Strike another blow for women's libbers!" he'll think. "Next thing you know this Earles fellow will be trying to convert *me* into a house-keeper." Which, of course, is not exactly true.

This chapter is not written to take potshots at husbands. The feminist movement and other writers have given us more than enough belittling material about the myriad failures of men. The last thing I want to do is give a wife who is fed up with her unhelpful husband ammunition for the beginning of family wars. Rather, I hope to spark the sensitivity of many men toward the daily pressures that irritate and frustrate their wives. As an insightful friend recently put it to me, "You know, Brent, our wives go through a whole lot as women—a whole lot more than we go through as men." Blessed is the man who understands this simple truth.

"I'm Doing the Best I Can"

Surely every woman has had her husband come home from work and ask the inevitable question of insensitivity at least once: "Honey, look at this place. What did you do all day?"

"What did I do all day!"—she feels assaulted emo-tionally—"I'll tell you what I did all day!" As if the con-stant stress she has battled the whole day long isn't enough, now she has to be tempted to commit homicide on her overexpecting husband.

Not being appreciated is a great source of frustration for some women. Being a homemaker is an extremely taxing job, but society gives off the mistaken impression that it's a piece of cake. A lot of us are gullible to the mental picture of the typical housewife as a simpleminded lady who stays at home because she isn't smart enough to have a career (homemaking isn't a career?). A homemaker is often visu-alized as a bit fat and sloppy, always in a frantic disarray; her hair is a mess; her house is a mess; she sleeps late and watches soap operas; she reads only the *National Enquirer.* And to top all of this, she's got a gravy job—housekeeper and baby-sitter. No wonder her husband expects everything to be perfect; he thinks she's got things easy.

I have a confession to make: I used to believe that ridiculous fable, too. What changed my mind? A few years ago I experienced what every man should experience at least once. I call it "Seventeen Days of Insanity," guaranteed to change a man's perspective on homemaking or else make him a first-class candidate for psychotherapy, whichever comes first.

My "Seventeen Days of Insanity" began at two o'clock in the morning sometime during the sixth month of my wife's pregnancy with our darling daughter, Sara. Jane did the most treacherous deed any woman can do to her man: she decided to have serious problems with her gallbladder, leaving me to tend house and a fifteen-month-old boy all alone. For seventeen days she vacationed in the hospital! Meanwhile, back at the ranch, I got the education of my life. Our little boy, Jared, was giving new meaning to the word *energy.*

The first day of my adventure was filled with all the novelty of proving my macho ability to switch over to "woman's work." After two days I had the hang of it . . . three days and I'd had enough of it . . . four days and it had the hang of me . . . five days and it hung me. About then, the doctors opted to perform some very delicate surgery on Jane. *How could she do this to me?* I thought. It had taken God five days to get my attention. Now the lessons could begin.

Lesson #1: Housework should not be a thankless job. If, after I had chased a toddler around for twelve hours while trying to straighten the house, somebody had said to me, "What did you do all day?" I would have clobbered him. When the world of dirty dishes, spills, fingerprints, phone calls, accidents, cooking, and washing machines became my domain, an amazing attitudinal transformation took place. In the quiet solitude of my thoughts, I could hear the echoes of complaints I had made to Jane. It dawned on me how cruel my mindless words must have seemed, spoken in the untimely and inconsiderate fashion that they were. I began to feel terrible that something so frightening as her emergency hospitalization had been the drastic measure God needed to get my attention.

The apostle Peter similarly rattled the cages of a few husbands in his day. At first glance it appears that he gave a lot more instruction to the women than he did to the men. But it must be remembered how the wife's role was viewed in that ancient culture. Women were treated as slaves and were not permitted the freedoms of expression and individuality that men enjoyed. So Peter's single sentence was a mind-blower to those machos:

> Husbands, in the same way be considerate as you live with your wives, and treat them with respect as the weaker partner and as heirs with you of the gracious gift of life, so that nothing will hinder your prayers (1 Peter 3:7).

Zoom in on two commands in that verse: "be considerate" and "treat them with respect." To a woman, this is how a man should demonstrate love and gratitude. The husband who only complains or takes his wife for granted is perceived as unthankful and unloving. If *your* cage needs rattling, listen to Peter. Or else God may get your attention otherwise.

Lesson #2: Wives and mothers need an occasional day off. Seventeen days seemed like a year to me, but Jane was accustomed to going months on end without a break. What a fool I had been to think she could labor endlessly and still maintain a strong spiritual life, a happy marriage, and personal sanity. What's worse, every time I visited her in the hospital I had to wonder if God put her there because he knew she needed a rest. Before the emergency, Jane's frustration level had grown very high, largely because of the pressures I was putting on her. Although surgery is never fun, she was able to recuperate wholly, not just physically.

When we read about the virtuous women in Proverbs 31, we find that she worked "vigorously" (v. 17). She started early and continued late—like many good homemakers do today. But verse 31 contains an important statement: "Give her the reward she has earned." Maybe part of that reward should include a shopping spree alone or a day each week at the local health spa. I found that "all work and no play makes Jane a crazy girl." Because I experienced it for myself!

Lesson #3: Boredom and loneliness are the occupational hazards of homemakers. Have you any idea how much time and attention a fifteen-month-old toddler requires? Enough to keep a woman isolated and busy for weeks. Being cooped up all of the time can be boring, no matter how godly a woman is. My encounter with insanity taught me not to fall for the traditional ethic about homemakers, which essentially says that a woman isn't supposed to get bored or lonely because of her job. One of the greatest frustrations a woman feels is caused by her obsession about being a good wife and mother. This paranoia plays tricks on her when she feels bored. She scolds herself: "You can't be bored! How can a good mother be bored? What's wrong with you?" Fast on the heels of boredom is loneliness, which causes even more false guilt because, after all, "a good little woman doesn't get bored with her children and crave outside friendships." Believe it or not, some inconsiderate husbands enforce this ridiculous and unfair doctrine of homemaking. No wonder some wives are so frustrated they could scream.

One of my favorite movies is *Mr. Mom*. The show is about a man who gets laid off from his well-paying position as an engineer for an automaker and becomes a substitute homemaker for his wife while she works at an outside job. You might think that the role reversals shown in the movie are a conservative's nightmare—score a point for the feminists! But that wasn't the movie's real message. I could really relate to the "Daddy turned Mommy" because of my own experience with trading places. From the time he poured a whole box of detergent into the washing machine and overstuffed it, to the time he was too late to stop the baby from eating a can of chili, I laughed and I cried and I said, "Yes, that's the way it is!" Jane just smiled appreciatively.

"I Can't Take Any More of This!"

Pastors sometimes get strange counseling situations. A few years ago I had what, up until now, has been my weirdest case. It started at about two o'clock in the morning (this must be an unlucky time of the night for me). I was asleep, but pastors also keep doctors' hours. You guessed it, a middle-of-the-night phone call. It was Larry, one of my church members. He apologized for waking me and then lowered the boom.

"Melissa and I just finished making love," he said, sounding a bit deflated. There was a brief space of silence, and I wondered if he was expecting me to comment. As you can imagine, this was a little awkward for me. Finally he went on: "And she just told me something you're never going to believe." Although he was dead serious, the manner in which he was telling the story had opened my thinking to some pretty humorous possibilities. But I shall never fully recover from the answer he gave me when I asked him what was wrong.

"Melissa just told me that she has joined the army," Larry said flatly.

"What?" I sort of chuckled.

He laughed, and I thought he was giving me a crank phone call. Then he said, "Really! She told me her bags are packed and she's leaving in the morning." He sounded too lighthearted, I thought.

"Larry, this isn't very funny. I'm trying to get some sleep." I looked at the clock, snapping back to reality.

"You think I think it's funny?" Now I knew he was serious. "Her bags are packed! She says she's catching the bus early in the morning. She said that's why she made love to me, because it's going to be a while before we see each other."

He was right—I couldn't believe it! But it was true. Early the next morning Melissa caught a bus to basic training. She walked out the door, suitcases in hand, leaving her husband and two young children to fend for themselves. The reason she gave revealed that her frustration had peaked out: "I can't take any more of this! I just can't take any more."

By now you must be thinking what I thought: "Then why did she join the army, of all places?" Well, Melissa had a plan. She needed a good job, but she had no education. The army was her ticket to an education, which would get her a job, which would pay for a comfortable and fulfilling existence, which would solve her frustration. But what about her family? Was she ready to let them go forever?

Unbelievable? No, not really. Unusual? Outlandish? Yes. But unbelievable, no. There have been many cases and varieties of AWOL. Pressures, stress, and frustration can cause a person to do surprising things. Melissa was responding humanly to, what had become for her, unbearable circumstances. Everybody does that in one way or another, or at least feels like doing it.

The psalmist had thoughts of this, and David speaks for us all:

> I said, "Oh, that I had the wings of a dove! I would fly away and be at rest—I would flee far away and stay in the desert; I would hurry to my place of shelter, far from the tempest and storm (Ps. 55:6–8).

Melissa didn't just *say* it; she *did* it! She found, however, that the army is hardly "far from the tempest and storm."

Soon, she knew how *Private Benjamin* felt. Not being able to run away from problems taught Melissa a good lesson: often *we* are the problem. After an emergency discharge, she came back to her family and responsibilities. Meanwhile, Larry lived an expanded version of my "Seventeen Days to Insanity." They both learned that you can run away, but you can't get away from yourself. Frustration must be faced head-on. Boot camp is a hard place to find that out.

"I Need Help Next Thursday!"

As Jane and I continued our ride home that Sunday evening after the church service, I began to think back on many of the concepts in this chapter, and I realized how easy it is to get wrapped up in our own little world and forget the struggles others may be having. Jane sat over there rejoicing, just because help was on the way next Thursday. There was light at the end of the tunnel!

Sometimes that's all a woman needs to ease her burden of frustration. The housework is piled up, every dish is dirty, clothes hampers are running over, the house is cluttered, the children are playing with a snake in the back yard, the dog just bit the neighbor boy, supper is burning—and Mother is frantic. Dad arrives home to this disaster and promptly sits down to read the newspaper. He barely says "Hi," but just reclines while Mom practices for a nervous breakdown. A slight hint of concern from her husband would be enough to spur the dear lady on. But, as it is, a fight of major proportions is brewing. Oddly enough, he rarely sees it coming.

Complicate this entire situation with the fact that many wives and mothers have paying jobs, which increases their strain and the likelihood of a shorter fuse on their tempers. The added frustrations caused by the wife's working outside the home are often not worth the second income brought into the family. To rephrase and apply something Jesus once said, "What does it profit a couple if they gain a great second income, but drive themselves crazy?" (See Mark 8:36–37.)

On Thursday I showed Jane how much I love her—I vacuumed the entire house. That night she showed how much she loves me. Husbands, a timely blend of understanding and helpfulness pays off (see the next chapter for more on that theme). Besides, can you imagine having to tell people that your wife left you to join the army?

6

Leave, Cleave, and Become One Mess

Two are better than one, because they have a good return for their work. . . . Also, if two lie down together, they will keep warm. But how can one keep warm alone? (Eccles. 4:9, 11).

No, this isn't specifically a book on marriage. What the world doesn't need now is another book about love. Preliminary inventory of the Earles library shows no less than twenty-two volumes on the subject of the still-problemed American home. So I'm not about to waste my efforts and your time by repeating the relationship-enhancers already expounded by other and better experts. As one Christian lecturer recently said, "Knowing what to do is not our problem; doing what we know, is." More irksome than the marital frustrations themselves is for a couple to know that they know what to do—and to know that they are not doing it!

Instead of listing several marriage-saving steps to "living happily ever after," how about if we discuss a few of the day-to-day trivialities that irk both partners into a frenzy. These are the dumb little things that augment arguments; these are the petty tricks and mindless head games partners use on each other; these are the adorable-turned-detestable traits that first attracted you to your mate; these are the underlying irritants that are hard to tell to counselors because they seem so insignificant. Trouble is, there are too many of them.

Before we actually get into the quirks and aggravations that most couples experience, let me say a word about what I call the "igniters." These are the countless fire-starters that arise in a household, depending on such things as the weather, how the day has gone, how many times this particular flash point has been reached before, and what mood your spouse is in. These igniters trigger fights. Here are some examples:

Dirty socks left lying in the middle of the bedroom floor
A depleted supply of clean underwear
Pet messes on the carpet
Not enough ice in the refrigerator
Spills
Untimely phone calls
Reckless driving
Forgetting to flush the toilet
Eating pretzels in bed
A ridiculously stubborn pepper shaker
Anything that breaks down
Overcooked food
Football on T.V. four times in one week
No dessert for supper
An unclothed bed at bedtime
Toys scattered everywhere
Unexpected company (especially a mother-in-law)

The list could go on forever. There are virtually hundreds of sparks that can get an argument started—sparks that ignite frustration into a fight that is even more frustrating. Since nobody is sinless, falling prey to rash behavior is inevitable. However, it can become infrequent if one practices the patience of a yielded spirit and an unassuming demeanor. Now for the things that really irritate. . . .

The Non-Communicator and the Blab

It has been said (perhaps unfairly) that a man speaks an average of approximately 11,000 words per day, while a woman speaks about 14,000 words. Estimations show that by five o'clock in the afternoon a man who has gone off to a job has already spoken over 75 percent of his words for the day. A housebound woman, however, has spoken only 40 percent of hers. Get the picture?

These figures may be a bit unreliable, but I can visualize the stereotypical home. In the last four or five hours of her day, the wife who has been at home catches up on her lack of adult conversation by using up the remaining 60 percent of her words. Naturally, being tired, her husband quietly listens, offering a grunt here and there. He will occasionally slip in a sentence or two, depleting what's left of his daily word quota. Some quick mathematics reveals that from suppertime to bedtime the wife does three-fourths of the talking. If this is anywhere near true, we shouldn't be surprised by the standard complaint of many women that their husbands never say anything.

Another twist to the frustration of non-communication is the stubborn refusal of a spouse to discuss and resolve a conflict. This can be done either passively or aggressively. The passive partner plays the martyr and takes whatever comes with the whimpering look of a mistreated puppy. The aggressive non-communicator clams up bullishly and may even storm out of the house, careful to slam every door.

A spouse may choose not to talk for a number of reasons. Often it's because it appears that the other person isn't listening and doesn't care about anyone else's opinion. Not having a golden tongue stops some from opening up. Since they expect to be "out-talked," they avoid humiliation by not saying anything. There are others who use the "silent treatment" as a ploy to get the upper hand in the marriage relationship, although this Jacob-like manipulation soon

drives a wedge between the two and leads to total communication breakdown. There are still others who think
that running away from the problem will make it disappear.

Good communication takes work. It requires partners to
accept each other instead of constantly trying to change
each other. Listening becomes as important as talking, and
a willingness to see the other's point of view supersedes the
meaningless and counterproductive desire to win the argument. When all else fails, love comes through.

The Neatnik and the Slob

Quite a few marriages are composed of one partner who
does everything decently and in order, and one partner who
sort of "goes with the flow." Usually the neatnik is also a
perfectionist and is therefore quite likely to label other family members (who don't come up to snuff) as slobs. Most of
the time, the neatnik and the slob adapt and get along well
with each other. But occasionally, when clutter and dust
have sufficiently agitated the cleanliness-is-next-to-god-
liness partner, fur is going to fly.

The neatness ethic is okay with the laid-back mate; it
just isn't a matter of life or death. In fact, the casual one
may not actually be a slob, but he or she is still a notch or
two below Captain Organized. Sometimes, when the drive
for tidiness becomes too persistent and the not-so-perfec-
tionistic partner has heard enough, even more fur is going
to fly.

We can laugh at this, and yet we've all been there. And
even though our squabbles and feuds start over the silliest
things, the pressure they create is exasperating because the
conflict of "a place for everything and everything in its
place" is one we know can never be completely solved. It's
one of those little areas in a marriage that comes up every
now and then, in which a couple needs to develop an understanding.

Having a territorial agreement can prevent many spats over who is messy and who is meticulous. For instance, it could be agreed that the living room, dining room, and bathroom would be kept spick-and-span by both partners. That would leave the kitchen and the family room for "creative expression." Each couple has to decide its own boundaries, but following fair guidelines can minimize needless frustration. Otherwise, the neatnik and the slob are likely to frustrate each other to the funny farm.

The Passion and the Prude

Christians are no longer ashamed to talk openly about sex. Have you noticed that? I think it's good. After all, sex *per se* is not wrong! Sure, there are some evil people who abuse sex in pornography, homosexuality, and promiscuity. But that doesn't mean we have to become ostriches and return to the pre–sexual-revolution days, when the subject was hush-hush. Why regress to the prior state of unsatisfying sex for one or both partners, when we now have the freedom to discuss marital intimacy and set the record straight on God's plan for couples?

Evidently the subject needs attention. A recent report that revealed the causes of divorce in Christian marriages cited sex as the number-one problem behind breakups. It seems that many partners disagree on the importance of sex to the marriage, which obviously *is* a debatable issue. Recently, however, I heard a sex therapist point out an interesting observation. He said, "Sex is not a big deal to the person who has a gratifying sex life at home. But to the person with a strong sex drive, if the couple's sexual relationship is not satisfying, sex is 90 percent of the marriage."

There are two extremes in sexual attitudes that trap many Christians. One extreme holds to the prudish Victorian ethic that says sex is for procreation only; it is a duty and not intended for pleasure. Although this viewpoint no longer has the widespread influence it had a few decades ago, it still lurks in the unconscious thinking of some good Christians. For example, I remember a counselor telling me about a couple he was seeing. When the husband complained of their poor sex life, the counselor asked if they were still having sex. "Oh, yes," replied the wife, "but we ask God to forgive us every time we do." Surprised? You shouldn't be. Since Scripture describes the "flesh" as evil, it's easy to develop the impression that sex is fleshly and therefore evil. Which, of course, leads to the errant belief that sex is okay if performed for reproduction only.

However, the wise words in Proverbs 5:18–19 are to the contrary:

> May your fountain be blessed,
>   and may you rejoice in the wife of your youth.
> A loving doe, a graceful deer—
>   may her breasts satisfy you always,
>   may you ever be captivated by her love.

This passage clearly has strong sexual meaning. It is right for a man to enjoy sex with his wife—even to be captivated with her charms. Husbands and wives should feel free to experiment with sexual delights in marriage. They have no reason to feel guilty or ashamed for enjoying their intimacy together.

The second extreme is what I call the "Christianizing" of sex. Some of the material I've read on intimacy in the Christian marriage causes me to envision a couple being romantic in a godly way (whatever that means), while an angelic choir strikes up an anthem over their bed. It's almost as if the partners are supposed to experience a "religious high" on cue with their orgasms. Pardon my candor, but it's this very idea that once implanted in the thinking, leads to sexual frustrations in Christian marriages.

Sex is just sex. That's all. Not an evil or filthy act. But not a religious experience either. It is fun and sometimes funny;

it is emotional and sometimes sacred and beautiful. Furthermore, sex should not be used as a weapon to give a husband or wife leverage to control the other partner. As Paul said, "The wife's body does not belong to her alone but also to her husband. In the same way, the husband's body does not belong to him alone but also to his wife" (1 Cor. 7:4–5).

Sexual frustrations occur for a variety of reasons. Since this is not a sex manual, I recommend that readers visit their local Christian bookstore and buy a book that deals specifically with such areas as romance, foreplay, stimulation, orgasm, erogenous zones, the menstrual cycle, impotency, and the biological differences in the sexual responses of men and women.

Remember, practice makes perfect. If your sex life is frustrating, practice! And don't expect so much out of sex. The key to sexual liberation for Christian couples is a let's-relax-and-just-love-each-other atmosphere. When the pressure comes off, the pleasure can turn on. Turn it on!

"Hellos" and "Good-byes"

Frequently a husband and wife end up barking at each other because of frustration buildup. Several external irritations gnaw at the two all day until, when they finally get together—even though they haven't done anything to upset the relationship—they're on the edge of tension. Suddenly and unintentionally, one frustrates the other, and it's off to the races! Sometimes, nothing needs to be said or done to upset the other person. The already-accumulated aggravations of the day are enough, and abruptly a spurt of red alert will be unleashed on the innocent spouse. This is better known as "Why are you taking your day out on me?"

Thoughtful "hellos" and loving "good-byes" can establish a positive frame of mind for a couple and avert unnecessary confrontations. An opposite example of what I'm talking about came from a woman who told me why she had reached the end of her rope: "Every day my husband comes through the door griping. If it isn't his job, then it's because supper is late, or the newspaper wasn't thrown, or he didn't like the lunch I made him. Just once, I wish he'd come through that door with a kind word!" Another wife described her husband's depressing good-bye routine: "He just gobbles down his breakfast without saying a word, grabs his lunch box, grunts or mumbles, and then goes out to the garage. Some days he doesn't even grunt or mumble."

Hugs and kisses start the day right and end it right. If considerate affections become routine for a husband and wife as they are coming and going, their time together or apart is more likely to start off on the right foot. The first thing said when arriving home, or the last thing said when leaving, often sets the stage for everything that follows. Proverbs 15:30 contains sound advice: "A cheerful look brings joy to the heart, and good news gives health to the bones."

Insignificant as all these details may seem, Tennyson puts it well in his *Idylls of the King:*

> It is the little rift within the lute,
> That by and by will make the music mute,
> And ever widening slowly silence all.

7

Life Without Money Trees

Whoever loves money never has money enough; whoever loves wealth is never satisfied with his income. This too is meaningless (Eccles. 5:10).

Someone has said that we spend at least 50 percent of our time thinking about money. That is, how to get it, how to spend it, how to save it, how much we need to buy this or that. We make jokes about wishing we had a money tree in our back yard, bedecked with an infinite number of pretty green leaves. Yet, if we did have one, most of us would pluck it to death in a week. We're like the guy who answered the famous maxim "Money can't buy happiness" by saying, "Yeah, but I'd sure like a chance to try."

In our society it's easy to get preoccupied with greenbacks. Jane and I have been experiencing this firsthand. We just bought a house. That says it all, doesn't it? This little adventure eats at the soul of a man, nagging him to pinch and count pennies at every corner. I'm surprised I didn't have nightmares during the ordeal of buying, selling, and closing. Imagine how terrifying sleep could get!

You know, there's no end to the ways they stick you for bucks in real estate—a title search, loan discount points, down payment, mechanical inspection, taxes, taxes and more taxes, mortgage insurance, deed insurance, home-owner's insurance, insurance on the insurance, appraisal fee, credit report fee, origination fee, recording fee, document preparation fee, notary fee, survey fee, and a final double-triple surtax. And you were wondering why I included a chapter in this book about money frustrations!

For house expenses, those are just the warm-ups. Next come drapes, paint, furniture, carpet, wallpaper, towel racks, extra cleaning supplies, flowers, and a bevy of other spiffy items to spruce up the new castle. Recollecting it all, I'm of the same mind as Joe Louis, when he said, "I don't like money actually, but it quiets my nerves."

House buying is only one financial leech in this money game. And I don't mean penny ante. Add cars, cribs, boats, bicycles, motorcycles, milk, doctors, dishes, utilities, underwear, trucks, toys, groceries, gasoline, food, fertilizer, on and on. It's enough to make a grown man cry. Who needs a money tree? A money *forest* would be more like it!

Here's the enigma that gnaws at me: last year most of us got along okay with less than we have now. Sure, we scraped and scratched, but we survived. Today, in many cases, we've got more—maybe much more—and we're in a bigger frenzy than before, which drives us to hunt even more of the green stuff. Say good-bye to another money tree. That old Chinese proverb hasn't sunk into us yet: "Everything you own means that much more trouble for you."

That may sound a bit cynical, but Ecclesiastes echoes a similar sentiment: "As good increase, so do those who consume them. And what benefit are they to the owner except to feast his eyes on them?" (Eccles. 5:11). Money calls for responsibility, and any responsibility carries a certain degree of stress. One has to weigh the heaviness of doing without some things against the pressures of having to earn more and more to stay afloat. Crazy world system! If you don't have enough money for anything but survival, you feel fustrated about making no progress; and if you're somewhere above the break-even point, your inner voice whispers that it will be disappointed if you fail to make more pretty soon. Jesus was right on target when he gave warnings about serving money and the spiritual distraction of riches.

No wonder we are told in Scripture not to get entangled in the affairs of this life. In fact, I love the way Paul writes it to Timothy: "No one serving as a soldier gets involved in civilian affairs" (2 Tim. 2:4). In other words, the Christian should not get wrapped up in a lifestyle that has nothing to do with his or her mission. If the lures of dollar signs become paramount, then some very miserable frustrations are bound to follow.

Debt

One expert has stated that "nine out of every ten people with an income are financial failures." That means most of us. His point is that because of mismanagement and poor financial choices, our bank roll turns into a donut hole. To play further on words, we make no sense with our dollars. Financial failure doesn't necessarily mean "going broke." Rather, anyone who is misusing money—missing the correct use of it—is being a bad money manager.

Don't be confused by the term *mismanagement*. It doesn't mean stupidity. Many of the people I have counseled about their money difficulties are college graduates with well-paying jobs. Lack of intelligence is not their problem; lack of understanding is. There are several ways in which people get their finances out of whack. Carelessness in any of these areas can have a strong negative impact on a person's fiscal fitness:

1. *Impulsiveness.* Proverbs 21:5 says, "The plans of the diligent lead to profit as surely as haste leads to poverty." There it is, right there at the end of the verse: *haste leads to poverty.* Hasty spending, my wife would tell you, is not one of my problems. On the contrary, I especially hate

being pushed to buy something on the spur of the moment. Recently Jane and I were doing some furniture shopping. We were expecting to make a significant purchase, and so I was in no big hurry. After considerable cost comparisons, we began to dicker with a salesman over the furniture we liked best. He took up more time than we had expected, and we had only a few minutes to leave and fulfill a prior commitment. When I told the salesman I felt we could make a deal but had to keep another appointment, he handed me a price quote and said it was a one-time offer. I said it appeared to be close to my budget but had no more time to discuss it that evening. Then he blew it. He said, "Mr. Earles, this is good for tonight only."

I replied, "You mean, after all this good-faith bargaining, you're telling me this price isn't good for a couple of days?"

"That's right." He sounded arrogant.

My blood was getting hot, so I gave him a "soft" answer: "Fine. Then it probably isn't good at all!" With that, I folded his offer, laid it on the table, and calmly walked out. Once I got outside, I grumbled and griped. Jane loves me, but she couldn't help wanting the much-needed furniture. For a moment, bless her, the hasty purchase seemed quite inviting.

Impetuous spending can be fun upon occasion, but careless impulsiveness can cause debts that will be an unwanted hardship later. It's what is familiarly known as "getting in over your head." With couples I know who have done this, one thing really dumbfounds me: they never do the logical thing to get out from under. Instead of adjusting their expenses by either returning or selling the penny-eating purchase, they further mismanage the finances God has given them by continuing to live beyond their means. Sometimes they complicate the buy-now-pay-later matters with even more impulsive spending. They don't comprehend that "later" means the spendthrift pays a big price in frustration.

2. *Miserliness.* Proverbs 11:24 says, "One man gives freely, yet gains even more; another withholds unduly, but comes to poverty." Just as impulsiveness can lead to financial problems, so can its opposite. Selfishness with money clogs up the channels that flow to financial freedom. The stingy person always comes to poverty. That doesn't necessarily mean that misers go bankrupt—there are other kinds of impoverishment. It is possible to be rich and poor at the same time. "Values" is what it's all about. What's valuable to you? If holding crispy greenbacks ranks high, then quite likely spiritual and emotional poverty are on their way. Perhaps miserliness is at its worst when a person withholds giving to God. Misusing finances in this way brings stress that brings frustration.

3. *Discipline.* The root of money mismanagement is an undisciplined approach to domestic accounting. Every financial counseling situation I've had related somehow to disorganization in the family budget. I remember talking to a couple who had no idea—not even a guess—of their monthly expenses. Sometimes they paid the bills and sometimes they forgot. Half of their creditors were ready to repossess. They were even two years behind on paying Uncle Sam. However, their monthly income sufficiently exceeded their apparent expenses. "How can that happen?" you're probably wondering. Plain, old irresponsibility. There comes a point when it catches up, though. And then recovery is going to be a long process. Proverbs 13:18 warns, "He who ignores discipline comes to poverty and shame. . . ."

4. *Laziness.* Some people are experiencing a money crunch because they're lazy and won't get a steady job. That may be abrupt, but it's true. The welfare mentality has warped the minds of some potentially industrious people and has promoted the rapid spread of the-world-owes-me-a-living thinking. Proverbs 23:21 warns that "drunkards and gluttons become poor, and drowsiness clothes them in

rags." A verse that parallels that truth adds, "Do not love sleep or you will grow poor; stay awake and you will have goods to spare" (Prov. 20:13). Those who are suffering financial woes because they prefer sleep to productivity cannot expect to escape the consequences.

5. *Scheming.* Do you know why some people have dollar difficulties? They are preoccupied with get-rich-quick schemes. They put their money in things that don't work and turn gullible ears to the sharp games of con men. One man I counseled had lost several thousand dollars in a jewelry investment that was "guaranteed" to yield him at least a 100 percent return. Proverbs 28:19 implies that we should not put our stock in lotteries, sweepstakes, and fast-money investments: "He who works his land will have abundant food, but the one who chases fantasies will have his fill of poverty." A man who keeps good accounts is one who has learned the long-term benefits of being a "steady Eddy." He works hard at his job and uses disciplined sense with his money. The results are God's blessings and the freedom from experiencing many of the frustrations that plague the careless.

Dependency

Money is a necessary part of life, an essential for existence. There's no way around it. What happens, though, is that sometimes we set our eyes on the end result—existing. We begin to worry about having enough money to live in the fashion to which we've grown accustomed. When we should be looking to the Lord for our security, we're tempted to trust only our weekly paycheck. Being paid regularly strokes our need to feel that we're doing okay. The longer this concept brews in our thinking, the more attached we become to the security of that paycheck. In our attachment, we become possessive and call the money ours. Actually, the money is not ours; it's God's. But our human nature has convinced us that so long as we have the money, everything will work out fine. This leads many people to spend themselves on making a living. All the while, they never learn how to make a life.

Eventually this becomes frustrating because, even though a person has money and should feel secure, true satisfaction eludes him or her. Remember the verse at the beginning of the chapter: "Whoever loves money never has money enough; whoever loves wealth is never satisfied with his income. This too is meaningless" (Eccles. 5:10). What's God trying to say here? Let me give you an Earles paraphrase of his words: "Money can't complete you as a person. The untold money-market certificate of satisfaction comes with casting yourself totally upon me. This includes not counting on your weekly paycheck to take care of you. Count on *me* to take care of you! Add it up any other way and your account shows up a big fat zero."

We need to rediscover our frailty and weakness. Earning money has an odd way of making us feel powerful and self-sufficient. But that trap is spiked with emptiness since it can't live up to its billing. Underneath our shining armor is a helpless child. The heavenly Father desires that we never forget that.

The prodigal son (you remember him, don't you?) thought his money was enough, and so he cried for his independence. But he soon found that the stuff spends fast. As frustration over his impoverished condition began to break him, the prodigal began to see where he could find the acceptance he craved—back at home. We are silly people who launch out in self-centeredness to discover that what we're looking for is back at the place where we started. A mouthful of independence tastes sweet for the moment, but once it's all been swallowed, what then? "Self" is singular, which spells a pretty lonely life. Lurking in the shadows are fear, stress, and worry. Don't you think it would be much easier to be dependent on something lasting, rather than independent? Our Father knows best.

Dependency upon God is to live life without money trees. Otherwise, you're liable to run yourself ragged trying to fertilize your financial gardens. Some people never learn. It reminds me of Mark Twain's pungent words: "Such is the human race. Often it does seem a pity that Noah and his party didn't miss the boat."

A few weeks ago, my son, Jared, gave me a good reminder about how God has blessed me and provided more than I need. We were discussing his appeal for money from me. Finally he said, "Aw, come on, Dad, you're rich."

Caught off guard by the cute innocence in his voice, I laughed and said, "No, Son, I'm not."

"Yes, you are," his tone sweetened. "You've got me." In that moment God reminded me that there's more to life than money trees.

8

Meet Me at the Bottom

I know that there is nothing better for men than to be happy and do good while they live. That every man may eat and drink, and find satisfaction in all his toil . . . (Eccles. 3:12–13).

Walt Disney is recognized as a man who made his dreams come true. But he started at the bottom. Disney once recalled his early days of failure: "When I was nearly twenty-one years old I went broke for the first time. I slept on cushions from an old sofa and ate cold beans out of a can." That's hard for me to visualize. The very name "Disney" sends pleasant pictures swirling through my head. I can see Mickey Mouse, Donald Duck, Pluto, the Love Bug, Bambi, Sleeping Beauty, Snow White, and a half-dozen other of Disney's screen creations making merry and bringing jubilant entertainment to millions of people. Somehow cold beans, a sofa-cushion bed, and Walt Disney don't seem to go together. But maybe that's what made him so successful.

Failing does one of two things for people: it makes them successful, or it makes them failures. Failing is the seed ingredient for either success or failure, depending on how an individual approaches a setback. It is possible to fail and not be a failure. It is also possible to succeed and not be a success. The secret of transforming failure into success is overcoming the fear of failing.

A high flier in the circus once described to Lloyd Ogilvie, pastor of the First Presbyterian Church of Hollywood, how a trapeze artist uses falling to become more daring. He said, "Once you know that the net below will catch you, you stop worrying about falling. You actually learn to fall successfully! What I mean is, you can concentrate on catching the trapeze swinging toward you and not on falling, because repeated falls in the past have convinced you that the net is strong and reliable when you do fall. The rope in the net hurts only if you stiffen up and resist it. The result of falling and being caught by the net is a mysterious confidence and daring on the trapeze. You fall less. Each fall makes you able to risk more!"

While the trapeze artist has to learn to capitalize on *physical* falling to become successful in his career, the majority of us have to recognize the benefit of *mental* falling to eventually triumph in ours. When things are not progressing as we planned, we inwardly miss the trapeze. This includes such things as not getting the promotion you have waited for so long; being offered a new job and cutback in pay along with a transfer, because the company you work for is being sold to another corporation; determining whether or not to join in your union's strike to receive wage and benefit increases; losing money on a "sure thing" investment that dropped in value; going bankrupt in your new small-business venture; sending your manuscript to an editor just to have it returned with a form rejection; or receiving a smaller pay increase than you had expected from your employee evaluation. The list could go on, but I think you get the idea: career frustrations are very real, and we must have a net beneath us that we can rely upon if we expect ever to overcome the fear and pain of falling. Only then can the mental letdown actually spark the pick-me-up that motivates us to keep believing that we can reach new zeniths in our occupations.

God wants us to enjoy personal satisfaction from our jobs. One of my favorite Scripture verses on the subject of work is Proverbs 22:29, which says, "Do you see a man skilled in his work? He will serve before kings; he will not serve before obscure men." This verse implies that it's honorable to shoot for recognition in our work. Of course, we are not to live for the applause of others, but that doesn't mean we have to earn their boos either. There needs to be a dignity within the fiber of a person that cries out for advancement.

Somebody asked me once, "What do you hope to accomplish in your ministry in your lifetime?" Big question. But there are some things I can answer to it. I was glad to have my chance. My response came as a surprise to the interviewer because it was more specific than the generalities she was used to hearing from others to whom she had posed the same question.

"First, I want to live my life in the will of God," I began. "When I stand before the Lord to give an account of my life's work, I want to be able to say I stayed within God's leading even though I adventured." I continued, "Within that framework, I hope to leave behind things that will bless people for many years. No matter how small or insignificant, I want to carve a mark upon society that says, 'Brent Earles was here.' But most importantly, I pray the work that outlives me will draw souls to Christ and challenge people to pursue God." I'm still working for that.

One of the reasons some folks don't reach any career goals is that they don't have any. You can't hit any targets if you don't aim at them. Since an occupation involves a large portion of your living, doesn't it make sense that you find fulfillment in doing what God has planned for you and giving your whole heart to being the best at what you do? Without that kind of purpose, frustration and disappointment will haunt you, because God created you for a specific task. To miss it is to miss satisfaction.

Alice in Wonderland contains a perfect illustration of what I'm talking about. Alice comes to a junction in the road that leads in different directions. Not knowing which way to go, she asks the Cheshire Cat for advice.

"Cheshire-Puss . . . would you tell me please, which way I ought to go from here?"

"That depends a good deal on where you want to get to," Chessie replies.

"I don't much care where—" says the wonder girl.

"Then it doesn't matter which way you go," grins the feline.

Don't get me wrong. I'm not saying you have to be on top to be happy. If the money trees from the previous chapter taught us anything, it was that having it all can be just as empty as having nothing. My point is, those who never find their station in life—who never become productive with their God-given talents—never fully taste life as it was meant to be. God has a design and destiny for each of us in this lifetime. This is what is commonly called "the will of God." If we don't care about God's will and are thus content to wander in any direction, then it doesn't matter what career we choose in this life—it won't count for much anyway.

At the risk of becoming workaholics, however, some striving souls are giving everything they've got to meet Zig Ziglar at the top. But they still land on their bottoms. What practical insights are available to the overtimers who have "plateaued out" and feel as if when they finally know the answers, somebody changes the questions? What can a person do to make guacamole out of a career's avocados?

Don't choose to lose. Not realizing it, some people unconsciously choose to fail. They do this in a number of ways. Some people are simply not interested in paying the price to succeed. They want promotion without production. Others have allowed pessimism to convince them that they are flops—so they stop trying.

Fear stops the fainthearted ones. It's what the famous psychologist Abraham Maslow calls "the Jonah complex." He said that even though we have an inner impulse to achieve (I believe that's what our Ecclesiastes verse is all about), we permit barriers to prevent us from translating our opportunities into realities. Maslow related this deliberate evasion of encountering potential to Jonah, recollecting how the prophet turned his back on the great opportunity God placed before him. How about you? Are you afraid of your talents? Have you subconsciously trained yourself to think upon success as unspiritual? Are you afraid of the dark side of greatness?

Another technique of the "won't win" crowd is to let bumps, bruises, and criticism kill their spirit. Underneath the occupational frustrations of hundreds of people is anger toward a boss, bitterness from being overlooked, or depression over someone's cruel remarks. Deep within boils a cauldron of self-condemning thoughts. In choosing to lose, they agree with their defeat by telling themselves, "See, I knew you couldn't do it."

Everyone was born to win. Unfortunately, many people give in to selfishness and pursue personal success apart from a spiritual plug-in. That's the ultimate way to lose. As James put it, "When you ask, you do not receive, because you ask with wrong motives, that you may spend what you get on your pleasures" (James 4:3). Check your motives. What moves you? Why do you want to win? Or why have you chosen to lose? Have you fallen into the net beneath your trapeze and decided to stay down for the count?

Don't compete to beat. Envious competition on the job is a major contributor to the stress and anxiety that accompany career frustration. Proverbs 24:17 contains an interesting piece of advice: "Do not gloat when your enemy falls; when he stumbles, do not let your heart rejoice, or the

LORD will see and disapprove and turn his wrath away from him." In other words, let God deal with those who attempt to intimidate you with comparison games and competitive confrontations.

When someone else receives the promotion you were hoping for, don't yield to the temptation to minimize his or her achievements in order to draw attention to your own. You don't have to beat others to become a winner. While healthy competition can be stimulating, combat is counter-productive, especially when the competitors start running each other down. It reminds me of the apt rhyme, "I hate guys who minimize and criticize the other guys whose enterprise has made them rise above the guys who criticize."

Play "80/20" and get plenty. Vilfredo Pareto, a noted nineteenth-century economist, believed that 80 percent of the production volume usually came from 20 percent of the producers. Apply this to your work and watch your productivity frustrations melt away! Invest your energies on the 20 percent of your ideas, products, clients, and methods that have proven to be fruitful in the past and test Pareto's theory. If he's anywhere near right, you'll have 80 percent of your plan finished in 20 percent of the time. Simple mathematics computes that out to be four-to-one odds in favor of efficient productivity. Not only will that feed your esteem the confidence boost it needs to conquer the frustration blues, but it may bleed over into other areas of your life as well. That means you may end up reordering your priorities. When you start hitting on all eight cylinders, your progress may become locomotive. Remember, God "is able to do immeasurably more than all we ask or imagine" (Eph. 3:20). Right? Yes, but don't forget the next part of the verse—"*according to his power that is at work within us*" (italics added for emphasis). We shouldn't sit around waiting for God to send our ship into the harbor. Maybe we should humbly call upon him to empower us with the gumption to go out and get the ship with a hard-working tugboat, before it gets lost at sea.

Let me close this chapter by relating the well-known story of the little boy who bought a new pair of ice skates, so he could play with his friends on the frozen neighborhood pond. Of course, his mother (doing what mothers often do) tried to discourage him by urging him to give up the skates, after she watched him crash to the ice every time he tried to get up on the blades: "Son, let's take them back before you hurt yourself!" Determined to stand up on the skates, the boy replied, "Mom, I didn't get them to give up with—I got my skates to learn with!" Good point. But you know what that means, don't you? Lots of falling. Meet me at the bottom!

9

Tying Knots in Your Ulcers

This only have I found: God made man upright, but men have gone in search of many schemes (Eccles. 7:29).

Guess where I am as I write these words. It's early summer in the Rocky Mountains, and the climate is perfect for relaxing. I'm sitting in the shade of an umbrella table, enjoying the sanctuary of tranquil Snowmass, Colorado. In the background, my children are trying to impress me with "cannonball" splashes as they do daring jumps into the sun-sparkled waters of an ideally heated swimming pool. Shortly, I will lay down this pen and permit the nearby, oversized Jacuzzi to soothe my tensions.

Our vacation hideway is nestled high above the village. Below us is a breathtaking, down-valley view. At the moment a pleasant breeze is romancing the aspen trees, while Jane and I have become submissive captives of relaxation. The whole atmosphere has so possessed me that it's a chore to write one sentence between long stares at the surrounding snow-draped peaks, which defy depth perception. Not that I'm trying to provoke you to envy, but don't I sound enviably unstressed?

Actually, our family had never before had a vacation alone. After reading some of the recent outbreak of material on the subject of burnout, I had been feeling my forehead to see if I was catching it. The sometimes breakneck pace of the ministry can eventually cook a person, like the frog who becomes a delicacy because he hasn't the sense to jump from a pan of water coming to a gradual boil. I love being a pastor, but it can be exhausting. The jokes about how a minister only has to give a little talk on Sundays are just that—jokes!

My pre-vacation months were enough to convince anybody that the ministry is definitely work. The apostle Paul suggested that we must become all things to all men, if by any possible means we may win them to Christ (1 Cor. 9:22). Becoming "all things," I have found, is a literal description of the pastor. Although I wouldn't trade the ever-revolving kaleidoscope of ministerial tasks for any other position, the pressures are no less demanding.

God has blessed me with a ministry that is at once invigorating and fatiguing. Naturally, a considerable amount of my time is dedicated to reading, studying, and sermon preparation. I suppose this responsibility swallows about twenty hours per week. Thank God, I like doing it! Of course, spice is what makes the ministry so delightful. And there are many shakers to pepper a week. Like staff meetings, administrative decisions, hospital visits, counseling sessions, daily radio broadcasts, Christian-school management, budgets, weddings, correspondence, emergencies, tragedies, funerals, board sessions, teachers' meetings, association conferences, special speaking engagements, church visitation, discipleship groups, teen rallies, summer camps, weekend retreats, and evangelistic crusades. All this happens with a hodgepodge of interruptions ranging from a member with a complaint to an unknown who needs something to eat. Somewhere between all of that, the pastor is supposed to eat, sleep, and cultivate a model family life.

Looking up from my paper, I can see scads of ski runs carved onto the mountainside above me, sweeping through the proud alpine evergreens. There still is a lot of snow in the higher elevations. The presence of the ski slopes, combined with the stress of the last several months, has reminded me of a story that fits the way I feel, and, for that matter, the way anybody feels who has finally gotten a breather.

A pretty skier was about to make her way down a challenging course in a competition for the handicapped. She was eighteen, and blind. An aide led her through the forty-four gates of the giant slalom and lined her up with the finish line. Then he yelled, "Straight ahead, go for it!" She was flying in her racing squat with poles tucked. (Some days I have a similar sensation. Preoccupation has me cruising full speed, blinded by the stress of the daily rat race, oblivious to where I'm headed.) Suddenly she hit a mogul. Now she was literally flying, as she let go of her poles and prepared to crash. Bouncing on her stomach, the bruised skier was still short of the finish line. (I, too, have had my days when I've gone sprawling like Mr. Agony in the agony-of-defeat scene of "Wide World of Sports" fame.) The skier knew she'd have to cross the finish line or be disqualified. She groped for her poles but couldn't find them. Determined to make it, the blind athlete started slithering through the fresh powder until she crossed the finish line.

The judge said, "You made it!" But her rustling ski suit and the crunching snow kept her from hearing him. She crawled another five, ten, fifteen feet, for all she was worth.

The judge was yelling, "Stop! You made it! You can stop!" But she still didn't hear. Finally he grabbed her and shouted, "You made it!" When it sank in, the skier jumped to her feet and whirled around for joy until she fell down again.

That's the same feeling I have sitting here. "I made it! I can stop for a while. I finally get to relax. I made it!" Ever feel like that? Like you've fought, and struggled, and crawled, and spent yourself completely, and now you get to escape from the moguls for a while? Everybody ought to know that exhilarating high.

Yet raw statistics and the demand for information on the subject of stress indicate that thousands of people are being slowly steam-cooked, only able to daydream about how nice it would be to break away from the strict regimen enveloping them. They want a bridge over troubled waters, but they don't have the time or energy to build it. They're reduced to going mechanically through the motions, secretly fearing that one day their emotional machinery may go on the fritz.

Stress is a monster. Recent studies report that stress is at epidemic proportions in our society. It's spreading faster than a juicy rumor in the underground circuit of a band of busybodies craving their daily fix of gossip. Healthwise, we're told, an inability to cope with stress can depress the body's immune system, lowering our resistance to colds and flu. More serious, it may influence the development of cancer. But that shouldn't surprise us, since everything seems to cause cancer these days.

Really, though, anxiety in the asphalt jungle can be tied to many physiological problems. Such as severe headaches, high blood pressure, strokes, asthma, and ulcers. Not to mention the frightening effect unresolved pressures can have on mental health. I'll tell you, I get "stressed" just talking about stress. Know what I mean? A few minutes ago I was sighing at Snowmass Mountain. Now I feel like the monster stress is laughing at me all the way from Kansas City and is plotting to munch on me when I get back.

Stress is inescapable. Most of the solutions for managing stress are simplistic, only temporarily treating the symptoms, while the real problem eats away like a vampire draining the last ounce of blood from his victim. As therapeutic as I've made swimming pools, hot tubs, mountaintop vacations, and uninterrupted relaxation sound, these remedies do about as much long-term good as a con man's cure-all elixir.

Speaking of medicine, stress figures into the popularity of America's three best-selling drugs: the ulcer medication Tagamet, the tranquilizer Valium, and the heart medicine Inderal. Unfortunately, many people are becoming dependent on pharmaceuticals to help them cope with the side effects of stress: anxiety, depression, and fear.

I realize that stress afflicts some people with shocking potency, and they require trained professional help. There are people who are as susceptible to emotional trauma as another may be to heart trouble. Stress is as dangerous to them as high blood pressure is to the other. But for those who are game enough to fight off anxiety attacks, three words comprise a spiritually proven plan of action: *admit, submit, commit.*

Admit your personal weakness. Huh? Flip back to the verse from Ecclesiastes that heads this chapter. See the last part? *"But men have gone in search of many schemes."* We think we're capable of handling so much more than we are. Granted, God designed us with an immense endurance for stress. But none of us is superhuman. And we shouldn't kid ourselves into a false, self-assured confidence that says, "I don't need anybody's help; I can face anything all alone." We have piously—stupidly—concluded that "good Christians" aren't supposed to feel frustrated and at their wit's end. So we learn to manufacture a victorious radiance before fellow believers, playing the role of the Tough Christian. Call it "the smiling-martyr complex." It's as though, if we cry for help and confess our utter inability to solve life's unscheduled cruelties, we lose face and fear falling from the ranks of those with fantasy-perfect lives. I've got news for you, there are no such ranks. God has no children who have mastered a dainty, upper-middle-class lifestyle with squeaky-clean happiness. But he does have many foot soldiers who conquered in the night because they realized in their grimy foxhole how weak they were, and they wept to admit it in humility. Then God came to them in all his strength, and they won a crazy, impossible victory like

Gideon's band against the Midianites. And, for the first time, they knew the meaning of "when I am weak, then am I strong" (2 Cor. 12:10).

Submit to the indwelling Spirit. Our inability to handle stress is a sure sign that we're depending upon our own strength and brilliance. It is surprisingly common for Christians to be ignorant of the significance of the indwelling Spirit. All too often we can detail the theological ramifications of "God in us," but never personally experience the healing, empowering, calming gift of the Holy Spirit. Have you ever gotten hold of this truth—not merely by fact, but by faith—that Jesus Christ alive in your body is his Spirit? Do you know what it means to submit to the greater-is-he-that-is-in-you power of God's Spirit? This message was always upon the lips and pen of Paul. But he said it no better than in Colossians 1:27: ". . . Christ in you, the hope of glory."

Commit your way to the Lord. This is an elementary theme of Scripture for the one who would walk with God, and it is crucial to getting free from the sticky web of stress, or at least seeing that web as the unlikely bridge that carries us to the next phase of God's unfathomable, flawless plan. Feel the goosebumps rise on your skin when David says in Psalm 37:5–6, 39–40:

> Commit your way to the LORD;
>   trust in him and he will do this:
> He will make your righteousness
>   shine like the dawn,
>   the justice of your cause like the
>   noonday sun. . . .
> The salvation of the righteous
>   comes from the Lord;
>   he is their stronghold in time of trouble.
> The Lord helps them and delivers them;
>   he delivers them from the wicked
>   and saves them,
>   because they take refuge in him.

Once we enter into this union with him—even if we must do it again and again—we can feel his love pulsing into our fears, frustrations, tensions, anxieties, and limp enthusiasm. Through the densest fog of our piled-high stress, we can see his way. And we have the assurance that it's safe to travel upon it, because he's already been there.

I just hope the first stop is Snowmass Village.

10

Batting .300 Against Temptation

Moreover, no man knows when his hour will come: As fish are caught in a cruel net, or birds are taken in a snare, so men are trapped by evil times that fall unexpectedly upon them. (Eccles. 9:12).

You have reached the halfway point of this book. Writing it, so have I. And for me this is turning into quite a lesson. Sir Winston Churchill once said that a manuscript can control its author like a mistress while he is preparing it. But *Bouncing Back* has become more than a mistress to me; it has become a startling phantasmagoria of frustration's myriad faces. My innocent investigation has burst into the discovery of an eye-opening subworld that goes on around us every day. All of us are touched by little bits of it without really noticing. These bits are the unexpected chuckholes of daily living that comprise the borders of this strange other world. Occasionally we come close to it, hit the holes, and have a biorhythmically bad day. Inside its borders there are stretches of time in which we are swept from the normal course of our lives. Then life becomes bigger than itself, and we are forced by frustration to think thoughts, feel feelings, and sense senses we usually never do in the day-to-day grind of "dog eat dog." During these intervals—"cruel nets" Ecclesiastes calls them—we may be mentally overchallenged, or physically pushed to the brink, or emotionally wrung out like a dishcloth, or spiritually carried to a pinnacle to be tempted or tested—or all of these things at once. The experience may not last long in comparison to a lifetime, but while it's going on, time seems not to exist.

We're in a fuss about nothing most of the time as we hurry through our busy schedules, and so we don't even realize how deep frustration can get in the subworld. Until it happens to us. While I was flirting with this mistress manuscript, playing detective with its theme, God permitted me to examine frustration by entering the subworld as others were experiencing it. He allowed me to touch their exasperation, and it was then that my mistress became my professor. I thought I knew something about frustration, so I could tell you and fix your problems. Boy, did I have another think coming!

If my description rambles with a philosopher's mysterious haze, it's not because I wish to lose you to sleep. It's because I'm grappling with my own understanding of what happens beyond the chuckholes, and why. Maybe it would help if I show you some of what I have seen. Care to look?

Over there lies a fine, young, Christian woman in a coma. She had planned to become a medical missionary, and had already been given hopes of receiving her training at the distinguished Mayo Clinic. While horseback riding, she accidentally fell off and was kicked in the head by her horse. Her parents, devoted Christians, began a vigil of prayer for their daughter. What agony. Eventually—miraculously— she awoke from the coma! But then came the grueling comeback trail of rehabilitation. Who can know the frustrations of this subworld except those who have been in it? The worst part, she later said, occurred during the coma, when she could hear people talking to her and about her, but she couldn't respond.

There lies another hospital patient, this one paralyzed by a stroke in middle age. Who can imagine the unexpected strange world he and his family were suddenly thrust into. I watched him struggle to communicate, unable to speak and with movement in only his left hand. For ten minutes, fifteen, he fought to have a single message understood, but no one could guess what he was trying to say. Then, with tears running across his temples and into his sideburns, he began to pound his left fist into the bed in desperation. That is the subworld I visited. Where life is survival, and survival feeds on your energy and courage.

Observe the parents of a young man who is dismantling his world piece by piece. His walk on the wild side would make even the prodigal blush. But sin isn't without pressure. Depression has set in, and emotional vertigo. Suicide, in its alluring glamor, whispers directions to a short, easy escape. He tries and fails. The despair swells. Will he try again? The chuckholes seem insignificant now, don't they?

Last stop. Do you have any idea what a woman goes through, she whose husband gets his jollies by coming home drunk and throwing her against the walls? Who worries about making it on her own, because she hasn't finished her high-school diploma? How will she raise two small children without a man? But tonight he busted her mouth and bruised her arms and legs. Tomorrow, while the rest of us fret over flat tires and leaky faucets, she will stagger through the subworld.

This is the heartache side of frustration. The battlefield. But what does the subworld have to do with temptation? Simply this: we don't combat flesh and blood and earthly shackles. Ours is a spiritual warfare. Even amidst circumstances that mock our very humanity, we are Satan's designated targets. In an unseen world, the demons and angels wrestle for the title deed to our spiritual lives. The tempter sends his hit men upon us with polished temptations, and he figures that the deeper our frustrations, the better his chances for making his mark. This is when we become most vulnerable.

A. W. Tozer, that unparalleled giant of Christian scholarship, knew about Satan's eagerness to catch us with our guard down. Listen to him as he explains that the Christian life is not easy:

> As we move farther on and mount higher up in the Christian life we may expect to encounter greater difficulties in the way and meet increased hostility from the enemy of our souls. Though this is seldom presented to Christians as a fact of life it is a very solid fact indeed as every experienced Christian knows, and one we shall learn how to handle or stumble over to our own undoing.

But this isn't a book on temptation; it's about frustration. Anyway, my point here isn't just that succumbing to temptation results in further frustration. The contrary. What I'm trying to say is that during times of subworld frustrations, we are susceptible to temptation we may at other times never consider. Think with me. What temptations crop up especially when life gets out of control and unpredictable?

1. *Unbelief.* In Matthew alone there are several examples of how desperate circumstances put faith on the rocks, and how Jesus pointed out God's ability to handle the worst of what we face. Above all, he immediately counterpressured the unbelief Satan was forging.

Check Matthew 6:30 in your Bible for future reference. Jesus is in the middle of his famous Sermon on the Mount, and he is dealing with worry, the by-product of doubt. Abruptly, with stinging truthfulness, he nails down the natural temptation that had gotten to the people of that day: ". . . O you of little faith." But, as he always did, the Master left them with a thoughtful, practical bit of reality to pump life back into their faith: "Therefore do not worry about tomorrow, for tomorrow will worry about itself. Each day has enough trouble of its own" (v. 34).

If you would like to trace the occurrences of weakened faith in Matthew's Gospel, let me chart you a course. Look up these passages: 8:26; 13:58; 14:31; 16:8; 17:20. You see, this is Satan's number-one tactic. He is not so interested in destroying *us* as he is in destroying our faith. By getting us to question our beliefs and God's sovereignty, he can render us quite harmless in the spiritual battle. And, in the sub-world, faith is one thing we can't survive without.

Consider the story of Allen Phillips. Maybe you've read about him. He was driving through the Grenella Pass, going from his home in Bailey, Colorado, to Georgetown, Colorado. Normally the trip would have been easy to make, but Allen got caught in a fast-rising blizzard. Having no chains on his tires, he was a sitting duck. In minutes he had driven into a storm that was drifting snow over the roads, and he knew he was traveling on a route that should be closed.

Soon Allen was hopelessly stuck. But he didn't panic or give up hope, even though he knew the frigid conditions would kill him by morning and he didn't have enough gasoline to keep the car heater running all night. That's when he came up with his S.O.S. idea. Allen began using his headlights to send Morse Code—three shorts, three longs, three shorts. He kept faith that somebody would see his signal and rescue him.

It just so happened that a Rocky Mountain commuter flight was overhead, and one of the passengers was looking out the window and caught a glimpse of the flashing lights. And it just so happened that the passenger could read Morse Code. And it just so happened that this passenger was the local deputy sheriff. He went up and told the pilot about the S.O.S. message he had seen. The pilot then made a swing around to double-check, and the rest is as you guessed. Shortly, two snow vehicles were dispatched from the sheriff's office to answer the three shorts, three longs, and three shorts.

That's an extraordinary story! It gives us hope that we, too, can hold on to faith in our worst times. Even when the greater temptation is to disbelieve God's power and desire to intervene. Once you learn to handle the curve ball of unbelief, you're on your way to batting better against all temptations.

2. *Blaming God.* Psalm 44 is a perfect example of the tendency of humans to blame God when all meaning seems lost. The psalmist starts complaining in verse 9, and continues until the song ends. Listen to the tension in verses 17–19 and 23–24:

> All this happened to us,
>   though we had not forgotten you
>   or been false to your covenant.
> Our hearts had not turned back;
>   our feet had not strayed from your path.
> But you crushed us and made us
>   a haunt for jackals
>   and covered us over with deep darkness. . . .
> Awake, O Lord! Why do you sleep?
>   Rouse yourself! Do not reject us forever.
> Why do you hide your face
>   and forget our misery and oppression?

You can relate to that, I'm sure. Satan likes it when he's able to lure this kind of emotion from us. Getting us to turn against God is part of his master strategy. So we must watch out, or else we'll fulfill the warning that is contained in the verse at the beginning of this chapter: ". . . so men are trapped by evil times that fall unexpectedly upon them." The temptation to blame God can trap us into selfishness and despondency. And once we turn against God, it's only a matter of time before Satan will dangle other tempting ornaments in front of us. At first to feed our ego; at last to steal our faith.

3. *Complacency.* The third clever device Satan springs on the distressed is the loss of will to carry on. Just today a man whose wife has filed for divorce commented to me: "I give up. I don't feel like trying anything anymore. I give

up on church, and the Bible, and God. I give up on everything. Nothing is any better, and nothing is going to be."
There you have the voice of complacency, the cry of "I no
longer care."

Isn't this what happened to Jonah? When God wished to
teach him mercy and compassion, using the rise and fall of
the vine he provided for shade, didn't Jonah rather choose to
be bamboozled by the devil's easier offer of pouting complacency? Sure he did. It's always easier to go that way—at
first. But if we never learn to hit Satan's curve ball of unbelief, or his fastball of blaming God, or his knuckle ball of
complacency, then can we expect to do anything but
strike out?

If you can't handle these main pitches, you'll never bat
.300 against temptation, which is a bad average anyway.
Without faith, trust, and hope, Satan will win. Not even
three shorts, three longs, three shorts can help then.

11

Flops, Blunders, Bloopers, and Goofs

Whoever digs a pit may fall into it; whoever breaks through a wall may be bitten by a snake. Whoever quarries stones may be injured by them; whoever splits logs may be endangered by them (Eccles. 10:8–9).

I have a confession to make: I'm a perfectionist. My Type A personality hasn't triggered any personality disorders, but sometimes it causes me to have unnecessary frustrations—the kind that Type B personalities rarely experience. Type B's are less demanding on themselves. They are also less demanding on others. Since they are able to adjust to a slower pace, they are less frantically goal-oriented, and performance alone is not tops on their self-evaluation list. They're not nearly as combative and competitive as Type A's.

On the other hand, if modern psychiatry could describe the Type A personality with one word, it probably would be "perfectionist." Type A's are self-sacrificing, overly conscientious, overdutiful workaholics. Due to their strict and rigid standards, perfectionists get irritated and impatient with people who can't keep up with their intense pace. In fact, A's and B's mix like piranhas and goldfish. And the result is the same if B's get too much in the way.

This inexhaustible inner drive is costly, though. Perfectionists usually are successful in what they attempt, but they rarely feel satisfied. Deep within they are pulled by feelings of incompetence, the fear of failure, and the critical anxiety that still more needs to be done. Thus, all actions come under self-scrutiny and all mistakes cause agony. The price tag? These obsessive-compulsives are sitting ducks for depression.

The shocking news is that over 75 percent of ministers who have been psychologically tested fall into this category. Doctors, lawyers, and musicians tested equally high. But why? I believe part of it is because of what society expects of certain people. We've put them upon crystal pedestals with no room for a blunder or goof. Let one of these professionals fall from his (or her) white charger momentarily, and he fears we'll never again allow him to wear the shining armor. Already possessing a bent to walk on water, he now feels he must prove he can. Of course, he can't.

Here's where mistakes play an important part. God can use them to remind us that we belong on clay pedestals at best, and, when riding, a quarter horse will do. If we get a notion to walk on water, we should sleep until it goes away, or else wait until ice-skating season. It's far better to accept our humanity than to pretend we're invincible; it's far better to rest in the overwhelming shadow of God than to imagine we're able to cast one of our own.

While some foul-ups seem to ruin an ideal plan, others are so humorous that they supersede the plan itself. A good friend of mine was out shopping with his wife when he got the sudden urge to jokingly arouse her jealousy. As she was standing at the cashier's counter with her back turned, he spied a mannequin facing in his wife's direction. How funny it would be, he thought, to sneak up behind this voluptuous, fake woman and call to his wife, while at the same time acting romantically affectionate with the tall doll. Brilliant idea.

"I still can't believe what happened," he confided. "When I put my arms around her, she was so *warm*. So . . . alive!" Talk about your big mistakes! He continued, "My wife turned to my call just in time to see me lock my arms around one of the customers! And it so happened that she was gorgeous! You should have seen the look on the blonde stranger's face when I told her I thought she was a mannequin."

I can recall making a similarly funny mistake in my youth, although it didn't get many laughs at the time. I was dating two girls from different high schools. Naturally, wanting to make a big impression, I did what every inexperienced Casanova does: I wrote them each a poem. Except! I wrote them the same poem, changing only the names to protect the innocent. What I didn't know was, they were friends and frequently exchanged phone visits. Fate would have it that they read their boyfriend's latest piece of literary prose to each other. Surprise of surprises! It was the same poem. And worse—the same boyfriend! But I was suave enough to persuade my favorite of the two not to give up on me. We've been married for several years.

Some mistakes aren't so cute and don't have such pleasant endings. Like the time I was in the hospital for knee surgery, and the nurse accidentally mixed up my medical chart with another patient's. Less than twelve hours after the operation the nurse wanted to take me to physical therapy to practice walking. Mind you, I was still reeling from the sodium pentothal and had a forty-pound cast on my leg. I told her she'd have to drag me down there dead before I'd go. She accepted the challenge with joy. And she nearly succeeded—in killing me, that is! I passed out in the physical therapy room and started turning blue. My leg swelled to the size of a tree trunk, cutting off the circulation to my foot. A couple of the therapists were slapping me in the face and dumping ice chips over my head to get me conscious. Of course, they stuck those nose-defiling smelling salts in my face, too. I awakened enough to see my orthopedic surgeon come bursting through the doors to the physical therapy room. He grabbed me up into his arms and shouted, "Who brought him in here? Who is responsible for this?" Then he rushed me into the adjoining room, which was decorated with many gruesome tools. He fired up a nasty little saw and sliced down the middle of my pretty new cast. This caused me no small pain, not to mention a setback in recovery. Incidentally, I never saw that nurse again. Sometimes mistakes are as costly to the perpetrator as to the victim.

For the perfectionist, few things are as frustrating as imperfection, whether it's someone else's or his own. When mistakes come—and they will come—they can ignite a forceful storm of anger. It's not unusual for a perfectionist to destroy an entire project or foil a whole design just because of one flaw or one kink. He may go into a fit of rage, throwing things, kicking the furniture, swearing, and then blaming anyone who gets in his way for his own error. Approval is what the perfectionist craves, and he thinks he can have it only if everything is exactly right.

Spiritually, life is deeply frustrating for Type A's. God is viewed as a demanding tyrant. His presence seems like that of an untrusting parent, and his voice shouts through the silence, "Do this! Don't do that! Straighten up! What's wrong with you? You'll never be a success! You can do better than that!" To Type A's, God is little more than a ruthless dictator from whom performance purchases grace, and perfection evokes love. It's no wonder they feel like a spiritual basketball—high then low, low then high, rebounding, dribbling, dunked!

A good passage for perfectionists to memorize and quote to themselves is Romans 7:14–20. In it Paul expresses his own struggle with failure. Although there is a difference between mere mistakes and the moral character of sin, all failures are related to our sin nature. When Adam fell—and the whole human race with him—attaining perfection became impossible. Listen to Paul tell it:

> We know that the law is spiritual; but I am unspiritual, sold as a slave to sin. I do not understand what I do. For what I want to do I do not do, but what I hate I do. And if I do what I do not want to do, I agree that the law is good. As it is, it is no longer I myself who do it, but it is sin living in me. I know that nothing good lives in me, that is, in my sinful nature. For I have the desire to do what is good, but I cannot carry it out. For what I do is not the good I want to do; no, the evil I do not want to do—this I keep on doing. Now if I do what I do not want to do, it is no longer I who do it, but it is sin living in me that does it.

In another passage Paul revealed the secret of immense patience, the power to handle flops, blunders, bloopers, and goofs: "Your attitude should be the same as that of Christ Jesus: Who . . . made himself nothing, taking the very nature of a servant. . . . he humbled himself . . ." (Phil. 2:5–8). Paul's message is *perfect:* "Live in total dependence on God's power; harness your strengths for serving others instead of racing them for self-glorification; and humbly accept your weaknesses that you may follow God's ambitions for you more than those you have set for yourself." Here are some other pointers that can help us avoid addiction to the tyranny of perfectionism:

Exchange the real for the ideal. One of the advantages of being a Type A is the ability to dream, to stretch toward unreachable stars. Type A's are racehorses who accomplish much more than the mudders around them. However, since they frequently confuse their dreams with reality, many of their expectations go beyond the realm of good reasoning. When one thus "quarries stones," he is likely to be injured by them. Both the real and the ideal must meet in our strive to arrive.

Eliminate all-or-nothing thinking. Everything is black-or-white to the perfectionist; nothing is in between. There are no partial victories. There is only one right way to do a thing, only one valid opinion in a matter, and only one correct debater in an argument. This is how it must be for the law of perfection to remain operative. If opposites can at any time, in any way, both be acceptable or lead to approval, there is no such thing as a *perfect* way to say, think, or act in a given circumstance. The perfectionist likes to keep all parameters of life simple, so mistakes will be easy to pinpoint. Of course, Christianity does have some absolutes: salvation is always by grace, Jesus is the only Savior for every sinner, and God is all in all. But while the absolutes of Christianity are foundational, the precepts of Christianity—which never demand all-or-nothing perfection—are functional. If we will humbly submit to God's leadership, we can fail and not be failures. Life is not always a matter of what is good and what is bad. Sometimes we must choose between what is bad and what is worse, or what is good and what is best.

It's bad to be imperfect, but it's worse to think we *can* be perfect. And it's okay to play jokes on one's wife, but it is never best to squeeze a living mannequin, especially if you can't laugh at your own mistake.

12

There Must Be More

*I have seen something else under the sun: The race is not to
the swift or the battle to the strong, nor does food come to
the wise or wealth to the brilliant or favor to the learned;
but time and chance happen to them all* (Eccles. 9:11).

Disappointment is Frustration's younger
brother. The two play in the same yard. Where you see one,
you'll see the other. I think it was Alexander Pope who
originated what he called another beatitude: "Blessed is he
who expects nothing, for he shall never be disappointed."
For if Frustration is Disappointment's older brother, then
Expectation must be his father. Nothing breeds letdown
like high expectations that can't be met, and nothing pro-
motes discontent in a person more than focusing on what
one doesn't have.

Saul of Tarsus was a man who had a lot of status, earthly
possessions, and personal accomplishments. In fact, the
name *Saul* in the Greek language means "big one." And
yet, what is recorded about him in the Book of Acts por-
trays a man full of hate and contempt. The first hint we
have of Saul's malice toward God's people is found in Acts
7:58. Stephen, one of the early church's first deacons, had
just finished preaching a piping-hot sermon to the Jewish

leaders. Being drunk with rage, they began to lay aside their garments. The men of the famed Sanhedrin planned to stone the unshrinking Stephen, and they didn't want their coats to hinder them from throwing their very hardest. This is when we're introduced to the subtle fury of the brilliant Saul of Tarsus: ". . . .Meanwhile, the witnesses laid their clothes at the feet of a young man named Saul."

Only two verses later, in Acts 8:1, the picture becomes clearer: "And Saul was there, giving approval to his death." How vicious! The rocks are pounding against the face and body of a God-fearing man, and Saul is cheering on the murderers. In verse three we see that he has taken up the brutal cause himself: "But Saul began to destroy the church. Going from house to house, he dragged off men and women and put them in prison." And then, a chapter later, Saul has become completely consumed with his mission of revenge against Christianity for replacing his beloved Judaism: "Meanwhile, Saul was still breathing out murderous threats against the Lord's disciples. He went to the high priest and asked him for letters to the synagogues in Damascus, so that if he found any there who belonged to the Way, whether men or women, he might take them as prisoners to Jerusalem" (Acts 9:1–2).

Saul, controlled by hate and ambition, became so driven that he lost all joy and peace. Disappointment met him on every hand, and frustration mocked him at every turn. His brilliance was not enough. We can assume that his expectations of Judaism were dotted with question marks each time he watched a Christian suffer and not lose faith in Christ. A storm was brewing within him, with its inner thunder rumbling through his discontented life. When Saul set out upon the Damascus Road, he was on a quest, but the greater search was taking place inside of him. There was more to life than malice, and Saul knew it. He was ripe for picking when Jesus converted him that day.

After Saul came to Christ, he had a name change. He went from being called "big one" to being called Paul, which means "little one." Everything changed about him, not just his name. Peace replaced misery, joy conquered hate, humility overtook ambition, and satisfaction swallowed up his longing. Paul's life became a clinical study of contentment. And today his words still throb with wisdom for those who are ungratified with life.

The Will to Lose

Winning. We're so enthralled with being first. How we loathe coming short of someone else's victories. L. B. Flynn cuts us to the quick in his potent book *You Can Live Above Envy* when he says: "The envious man feels other's fortunes are his misfortunes; their profit, his loss; their blessing, his bane; their health, his illness; their promotion his demotion; their success, his failure." What is wrong with us that makes us feel we must be ahead of others all the time?

Let me hasten to say that goals and accomplishments are not a bad thing. I have met some Christians who have no spunk and consequently displease the Lord. Burying talents is a surefire way to arouse God's disfavor. We must be hardworking, faithful stewards. But we are not serving God when our achievements come at the expense of others' failures.

Real satisfaction is derived from practicing a principle that rises above the get-ahead-and-stay-ahead philosophy. It's what Paul might have termed "the will to lose." This is more than a willingness; it's a determination. The disciple must learn to lose every earthly thing if he would plunge into the deep sea of contentment.

> But whatever was to my profit I now consider loss for the sake of Christ. What is more, *I consider everything a loss* compared to the surpassing greatness of knowing Christ Jesus my Lord, for whose sake I have lost all things. I consider them rubbish, that I may gain Christ . . . (Phil. 3:7–8, italics added).

Christ is our contentment. Nothing else satisfies. And if we are not determined to put aside the things of this temporary place, we will not know the excellence of his eternal satisfaction poured into our everyday cup. What disappointment must follow the man whose cup never runneth over! Saul searched for this and never found it. But Paul did.

Contentment Is Not Complacency

Hebrews 13:5 tells us: ". . . be content with what you have. . . ." The term used here for "content" conveys the idea of "That's enough; that's sufficient; that will do." Tremendous outlook. But isn't it sort of a devil-may-care attitude? Not really. A contented person is not a complacent person. Being nonchalant and self-satisfied is not the same as contentment. Complacent people are unaware of life's tough challenges and unconcerned about improving on their own weaknesses.

Many years ago the famous comic strip of *Mutt and Jeff* drew a similar contrast between contentment and complacency. Jeff was snoozing under the shade of his favorite tree. Mutt came up and said, "Jeff, why don't you get up?"

Jeff replied groggily, "Why?"

Mutt said, "So you can get a job."

Jeff answered, "Why?"

Mutt said, "So you can make some money."

Jeff shrugged, "Why?"

Mutt said, "So you can save it."

Jeff asked, "Why?"

Mutt said, "So you can get a lot of money."

Jeff asked, "Why?"

Mutt said, "So you can retire someday."

Jeff asked yet again, "Why?"

Mutt barked, "So you can just lie around and do nothing."

Jeff replied, "Why, Mutt, that is what I'm doing now. Why go to all the trouble?"

Though Jeff may appear to illustrate contentment, he actually was merely complacent. To be content does not mean we stop caring or quit trying to do better. Contentment does not make us roll over like a wet worm after a rainstorm. It merely means that we are satisfied to live life today with the strength and blessings God gives us. But even in that satisfaction is a passion to reach beyond ourselves to something greater—for God's glory! Saul, ambitious as he was, hunted for this. Paul learned it and lived it. Listen to his words:

> Brothers, I do not consider myself yet to have taken hold of it [perfection]. But one thing I do: Forgetting what is behind and straining toward what is ahead, I press on toward the goal to win the prize for which God has called me heavenward in Christ Jesus (Phil. 3:13–14).

There's nothing complacent about that kind of living. Note that Paul said this only verses after stating his determination to know Christ rather than to have status. A few verses later, in chapter four, he teaches us lesson number three.

Striving to Arrive

Contentment is completely devoid of pressure, panic, inner turmoil, and greed. It is one thing to be in pursuit of Christ and the will of God (as Paul said in Phil. 3:13–14), but it is quite another thing to be driven to the brink of a nervous breakdown in search of success, as many worldlings are. Contentment is often equated to attainment: the more we attain, the more content we will be. But that isn't true.

Doctors, lawyers, corporate executives, and other workaholic professionals (remember those Type A's?) are among those who most frequently seek psychological counseling for stress-related problems, and they also rank high in suicide statistics. On a recent trip I met a corporate executive who was involved in psychiatric therapy. He said he felt like the Irish fisherman who couldn't get his rope on the boat because somebody had cut the end off. His eyes still frowned with anxiety when he told me, "I found that climbing the corporate ladder didn't satisfy. It only created pressures I hadn't planned to handle. I had more money, a bigger home, fancier cars, and prime investments, but less happiness and no peace."

Paul could have told him that. Contentment is learned, not earned. As you read the apostle's words, bear in mind that as Saul of Tarsus he was on his way to worldly success. Still, disappointment haunted him. Later he would escape the clutches of frustration by learning to accept that even disappointment is a part of growing in grace. Listen to him tell it:

> . . . I have *learned* to be content whatever the circumstances. I know what it is to be in need, and I know what it is to have plenty. *I have learned the secret of being content* in any and every situation, whether well fed or hungry, whether living in plenty or in want (Phil. 4:11–12, italics added).

Did you catch that? The secret of being content. What is it? Paul teaches us in the next verse: "I can do everything through him who gives me strength" (Phil. 4:13).

That is the secret to contentment. We do not strive to arrive, but the power of Christ becomes our inner drive.

The Thrill of Emptiness

Disappointment is the result of coming short of something that was highly desired or expected. For people who are preoccupied with being full, disappointment is inevitable. The hardest lesson of contentment is also the most important: to be consistently content we must imitate Christ. This truth is the final link in Paul's seminar on contentment as it was given to the Philippians.

In Philippians 2:5 the apostle tells Christians to have Christ's attitude, and then he describes that attitude in the following verses. But verse seven is the key. It is here that we find the great "kenosis" reference to Christ. *Kenosis* is the Greek word Paul used to describe the humble act Christ did in becoming God in human flesh. As the beginning of the verse translates it, Christ "made himself nothing." That's kenosis! It means "to pour out, to empty." Christ poured himself out and became humble.

To really be filled we must have learned the thrill of emptiness. In pouring ourselves out for others, like Christ did, our cup becomes empty. Then we can honestly come to God in prayer, asking him to refill it. As that cycle continues we experience genuine contentment. There is lasting satisfaction in self-emptiness, and even greater gratification in God's refilling grace.

And the end of your rope is never cut off. Although you'll probably never need it.

13

Silent Night, Sleepless Night

There is a time for everything, and a season for every activity under heaven: . . . a time to weep and a time to laugh, a time to mourn and a time to dance (Eccles. 3:1, 4).

I shall never forget the field trip our class took when I was a young seminarian in Pastoral Theology. Would you believe we toured a funeral home? It was quite a learning experience. The undertaker and our instructor led the tour, explaining everything we always wanted to know but were afraid to ask about funerals. As they alternated back and forth in a candid unveiling of the secrets of death and burial—one told the ins and outs of conducting a proper funeral, the other interjected how to best minister to the bereaved at the graveside and afterwards—I could feel myself being drawn into the lesson by my own fascination with death. Yes, you heard me right. Fascination with death is natural, I think. For, as the German theologian Helmut Thielicke wrote: "Every attempt to get at the meaning of life must inevitably face the question of death."

To this day, though, I wonder about my normalcy, because one part of the tour was particularly intriguing to me. I hope you don't think I'm weird, but I was enthralled with the embalming room, especially since there were people being embalmed there. The funeral director described in detail the entire process, pointing out the various procedures on one of the corpses. Everything was very sanitary, and, of course, the smell of formaldehyde permeated the room. Evidently it was all too much for my partner, who had become quite still and unusually white. When he took a step backward and bumped into the body that was next to be embalmed, the instructor had to help him out of the room. At the moment it was sort of humorous, but I realize now that it perfectly illustrates that not only are we fascinated with death but we are afraid of it. Perhaps even sickened if we come face to face with it.

Not coming to grips with our own feelings about death leaves us unprepared to handle grief therapeutically. We end up feeling lost within ourselves, shocked by the surprise of death, and uncertain about our understanding of death itself. It is very important for the believer to resolve some questions about death. Why do some people die what appears to be a premature death? How should I view death in the cycle of life? Am I prepared for my own death? My spouse's? My children's? These questions and others should be considered beforehand and settled by God's Word.

Death must be seen as a natural part of life. It is the ultimate reality. This does not mean we should not feel sadness at the death of a loved one; it simply means we are to accept death without confusion, since it is as much a part of the life cycle as eating food. Having the assurance that death is natural—even admitting, "One day I am going to die"—is the first step to developing a healthy outlook on death. Otherwise we're likely to have an Elijah-concept of "passing on" (see 2 Kings 2:11): "Only chariots of fire could take me or my loved ones away." With that attitude, we accept the subtle subconscious creature-pleaser that whispers, "Death touches everyone else's family but not mine." The result is, we are so stunned by death when it comes that we cannot grieve freely. Why? Because we have not come to grips with our feelings about death.

Grief is complex. If you don't believe me, just try to define it. Grief encompasses so many feelings that it's hard to put into words. This simple definition might help us get a handle on it: *Grief is the emotional struggle a person goes through at the time of a loss.* It is normal and inevitable. And usually it is a mostly negative feeling. Does that surprise you? It shouldn't. In preparation for writing this chapter, I studied the various Greek and Hebrew words used to express "grief" in the Scriptures. After looking at dozens of verses and extra-biblical uses of the same words, four emotions surfaced in connection with the experience of grief: pain, misery, anger, and fury. Those are all negative.

This complicates things for Christians, because we are led to believe it isn't right to have negative feelings. Godly people are always supposed to be on top of their game. They can't show hurt. They can't be miserable. They can't be mad. They can't have furious outbursts. Positive thinkers may preach that baloney, but Jesus did not: "Blessed are those who mourn, for they will be comforted" (Matt. 5:4).

Jesus himself grieved and dealt with the grief of others. He mourned the death of Lazarus (John 10); cried over Jerusalem because she denied him to be her Messiah (Matt. 23:37); was distressed at how his Father's house had become a den of thieves (Mark 11:15–17); sought support from his disciples, who were "exhausted from sorrow" (Luke 22:45); comforted his disciples when they were filled with grief (John 16:6, 20–22); poured out sweatdrops of blood in anguish (Luke 22:44); and looked after his grieving mother as she beheld his death (John 19:26–27). No wonder Isaiah described him years before his incarnation to be "a man of sorrows, and familiar with suffering . . ." (Isa. 53:3). In working through the negative feelings of grief, Jesus taught us that the best way to handle heartache is to allow ourselves to have emotions, even negative ones. To bounce back from the frustration of grief, we must not rush, ignore, or delay our sorrow. When we release pent-up emotions, we find the psalmist's words to be true: ". . . weeping may remain for a night, but rejoicing comes in the morning" (Ps. 30:5).

Grief comes in many degrees and for varied reasons. We know that death is the most obvious cause of grief, but there are other types, too. For example, parents feel grief of a sort when their first child goes to school, when their children graduate, and when the last child leaves home. There is grief when an eye or limb is lost, when a child runs away or is abducted, when health fails or surgery is necessary, when a financial setback is experienced, when a divorce divides the family, when one is the victim of a crime, when a job is lost by firing or layoff, when a sentimental treasure is stolen or destroyed, and even when a pet dies.

After we acknowledge the negative feelings of grief, and accept that it's okay to feel them, there are some other things that may help us face the hurt:

Be aware of the stages of grief. Before I mention the different reactions we have to grief, let me emphasize that no two people go through these stages in the same order and at the same rate. Usually the initial stage is *disbelief.* It is only natural that we protect ourselves from pain, and a sense of numbness shields us from the immediate sensation of loss.

The outpouring of emotion normally comes later, and it's important that we cut loose our anguish, or we may not bounce back at all. As frustrated and helpless as grief may leave us, it is necessary to work through the misery. The Old Testament Hebrew did this by tearing his clothes off, wearing sackcloth and ashes, and wailing in agony. That is perhaps a bit melodramatic, but it's better than hiding the hurts underneath an expressionless exterior.

Deep distress is part of the process, too. Mourning people may become recluse, lonely, and depressed. It's not uncommon for the bereaved to become physically exhausted, unable to function. During this stage, hostile resentment may surface, and the sufferer may try to blame somebody, including God, for the death of the loved one. Guilt may surface, too, especially if the relationship with the loved one was incomplete before death came. Such forms of distress last for a while and require the loving assistance of others long after the kind visits and words of friends and relatives are over.

Finally, *hope for resuming life* begins to return. Don't expect this to come quickly. It takes time to relive old memories, plan for the future, and consider the hope of eternity for a loved one. But, thank God, we believers do not "grieve like the rest of men, who have no hope" (1 Thess. 4:13).

Eventually—gradually—we *readjust to life.* And yet, this does not come easily. Making new relationships and returning to reality can be very difficult. Still, there must come the healing point where we determine within ourselves to meet every discouragement with courage.

Talk openly about death and grief. Many of us don't know how to do this. As close as we may be to someone who is grief-stricken, we are usually panicked about what to say. I don't know how many times I've heard people comment: "I feel so awkward talking to her. I just don't know what to say." Certainly, there are no magic words that make the hurt go away, so don't worry about learning them.

As long as we avoid asking foolishly obvious questions (like "This is difficult for you, isn't it?") and avoid Christianized platitudes (like "Well, we know he'll be better off where he is," or "The Lord giveth and the Lord taketh away—blessed be the name of the Lord"), we can approach our bereaved friends and relatives openly. Depending upon how well we know the mourners, we can best help them deal with grief by talking privately with them about their loss. Likewise, we ourselves mend better when we talk honestly about our pain with those who care enough to listen.

I remember visiting a funeral home to see one of my dear friends the evening before the funeral of his father. While others milled about, renewing acquaintances and viewing the body, he and I sat at the back, talking about our memories of his father. At first, he was surprised to hear me talking about his dad as if he were alive, reliving humorous events and his father's distinctive traits. But soon he joined in, and we both laughed to remember some of the things. We cried, too, because the cancer had come so swiftly. Before I left, he embraced me solidly and didn't let go for the longest time. I knew our friendship had ventured to a new depth. It was in our eyes. Honest, open talk does that for people.

Recognize God's presence. In a recent poll, George Gallup found that more than half of the Americans experiencing grief turn to God, prayer, and Scripture reading for comfort. Of those who do, 94 percent said it is highly effective. We knew that, didn't we? Few things help a mourner like the reassurance that God still loves and cares for his children. Even when we do not feel God's nearness and do not know how to pray, we can hold tightly to the promise of God: "In the same way, the Spirit helps us in our weakness. We do not know what we ought to pray for, but the Spirit himself intercedes for us with groans that words cannot express" (Rom. 8:26). We can tell God everything; he already knows how we feel. Or we can just cry. He understands.

Minister to the grieving. This is a sure way to be helped in your time of grief. The Scripture promises: "Blessed are the merciful, for they will be shown mercy" (Matt. 5:7), and "Give, and it will be given to you. A good measure, pressed down, shaken together and running over, will be poured into your lap. For with the measure you use, it will be measured to you" (Luke 6:38). Think about that when you consider the bereaved people around you.

"But how can I minister to people who have lost a loved one?" you may be wondering. Three things can serve as a guideline to help you:

1. Keep contact with them. Effectiveness takes time.

2. Talk about the loved one who has died. It's even good to mention the person by name.
3. Invite your friend to outings when the time seems right. Your stabilizing presence will make it bearable.

Maybe grief teaches us truths we could never learn any other way. Truths like the one contained in John Masefield's words:

> And God who gives beginnings
>   Gives the end;
> A place for broken things
>   Too broke to mend.

In the few days it took me to write this chapter, I paused to talk to a friend who is just recovering from the death of his mother (which occurred nearly a year ago), to pray with a dear woman who is adjusting to her husband's massive stroke, to advise a woman whose daughter is addicted to cocaine, to counsel three different individuals facing divorce, to encourage a member who was laid off from his job, and to lend support to a lady struggling with a crumbling marriage. Just before I wrote this last paragraph, I rushed off to the hospital to pray with an expectant mother who was taken in for an emergency mastectomy. As I waited at one of the stoplights near the hospital, a funeral procession passed through. It reminded me of how many people face the pain of grief every day. For thousands, tonight will be a silent night—and a sleepless one.

14

Variations of Solitaire

If one falls down, his friend can help him up. But pity the man who falls and has no one to help him up! (Eccles. 4:10).

Being single is not so unusual. Not anymore. Over 40 percent of all Americans over the age of eighteen are single. Four out of ten. And 85 percent of those single people are aged eighteen to sixty-five. You may be surprised to know that the greater percentage of singles are over thirty.

Here's another not-so-unusual modern status: being a single parent. The growing divorce rate of the late seventies and early eighties has made single-parent homes a new reality for the contemporary church to face. In fact, sociologists estimate that at least 45 percent of American children will live in single-parent homes by 1990. That's almost half!

Still, there is a unique frustration that accompanies aloneness. That thousands of other people are also alone doesn't make you feel less alone. My wife and I have frequently had single people over for dinner or fellowship. After establishing relationships with some of them, we have learned what sort of emotional struggles they go through, even the ones who have accepted their singleness as God's will. Perhaps the strangest feeling many singles face is that of being a "third wheel" in social situations. Though it's common for a single person to feel like the "odd man out," singles want and need good friendships with strong Christian families.

There are all sorts of variations of solitaire. Let's consider them before we get down to the nuts and bolts of how single people can bounce back from the frustrations peculiar to their way of life. There are at least six styles of singleness:

The young single. Nothing out of the ordinary here. Most college students aren't married. As a matter of fact, most of them aren't interested in marriage—yet! These people are too busy changing their majors, getting job placement, enjoying their independence, playing the field, and philosophizing about how to solve the world's problems to get married. Love is on the way, someday, they figure. So most of them are only moderately aggressive about doubles. For now, singles is enough.

The career single. By that I don't mean someone who has made a career out of being single. This is a person who has passed the preppie, Rah! Rah! stage, and has begun to settle down. Often this is a very responsible, very busy person. Being responsible and busy helps. Career-aged singles sometimes become workaholics because their work becomes their identity, and then they don't have much time to think about being alone. Underneath the poised exterior, though, lurks an occasional probing curiosity about how much longer Cupid is going to take.

The older single. Society is not very courteous with its labels for those who never married. Thus, a spooky fear may creep into the emotions of a single person in his or her early thirties when hearing that less than 5 percent of couples getting married are over the age of thirty-five. A weird sense of panic begins to set in. Words like "spinster," "old maid," or "confirmed bachelor" have a nasty ring to them. Even if you never hear such things said about you, an inward, private paranoia suggests that others are at least whispering them behind your back.

The divorced single. The church is just starting to understand the suffering these people are going through. It sickens me to see greeting-card companies manufacturing "divorce cards" with sarcastic humor, but it illustrates that there is a large segment of our population in need of encouragement. Unfortunately, they have become a sizable market, and unethical businessmen will try to capitalize on their pain or bitterness. For sure, the church needs to start doing a better job of ministering to divorced people. I recently received a letter from a Christian man who had gone through a divorce, and he felt that his church either didn't know how to minister to him or didn't care. In one portion of the letter, he puts his finger on the need for Christians and churches to awaken to a nonjudgmental ministry of restoration for divorced singles:

> . . . . First of all, divorce is humiliating, emotionally and spiritually draining, and horrible overall. I never want to go through it again as long as I live. When a divorce occurs, the person going through it needs a lot of prayer and encouragement. For the most part, Christians and pastors don't have any idea of how to minister to a person who is going through a divorce, or who is divorced. While many Christian marriages are ending in divorce, most evangelical churches turn a blind eye to the issue. During the time I was going through my divorce, and since my divorce became final, I haven't found a single evangelical church, or pastor, who really understands the emotions caused by a divorce. About all I got was sympathy. There was no one to minister to me who really, and truly, understood what I was going through. I believe many Christians are lost to the world because of divorce. Their spouses reject them, then, when they turn to their home churches, all they find is coldness and apathy. Several people at my home church asked some very cruel,

personal questions during this time, which did me much more harm than good.

I really believe that, sooner or later, evangelical churches are going to have to deal with the divorce issue. When divorcing, or divorced, Christians find rejection in evangelical churches, they will turn to liberal churches where they are welcomed with open arms. . . . Let's face the facts, would you continue in a cold and threatening environment if you were hurting, or would you turn to someone who offers you a shoulder to cry on, and supports you at your darkest hour?

How's that for getting straight to the point? Considering that divorced singles also often become single parents, the frustrations are further complicated.

The young widow or widower. We do not realize how many young men and women re-enter single status because of a tragedy. The obituary columns give us reports of young people who have lost a spouse far too often. Not only is this person left with the frustration and depression of his or her personal grief but also suffers the pain of being single once again—and often children may be involved. The road to recovery is a grind, not only because of the grief, but also because of the unaccustomed aloneness.

The older widow. We almost expect this, since women usually outlive their husbands. That's a proven fact. We expect to hear of grandmas who become single again. And we don't expect them to remarry. Not that we oppose it; we just don't expect it, particularly if they were married for a long time before widowhood. Often remarriage is not in the picture. Especially if the widow (or widower) has financial security, grown children, and playful grandchildren to fill the days. Nonetheless, there is an emptiness that accompanies being an older person who became a single by losing a spouse.

Each of these types of single people have a set of problems unique to their kind of singleness. For instance, the young single has an entirely different set of obstacles and frustrations from those of a young widow. And yet, both of them are single. Therefore, it is difficult to address the needs of each in one chapter. I do think this is valuable information, though, because it can awaken the Christian community to understand the need and do something about it. More effective than books or chapters is a church full of compassion and warmth to welcome these people into the *family* of faith.

Meanwhile, there are some basic scriptural principles that speak to all singles alike:

You are not alone. You may feel lonely, but you're not alone. Hebrews 13:5–6 says: ". . . be content with what you have, because God has said, 'Never will I leave you; never will I forsake you.' So we say with confidence, 'The Lord is my helper; I will not be afraid. . . .'" I am not going to condemn the feelings of loneliness you may have, because they're a natural part of being single. The word *single* itself carries the aspect of aloneness. But while you may be physically alone, God is with you.

I realize God cannot play Parcheesi with you or join you in watching your favorite T.V. show. But he does understand the feelings of your infirmity (Heb. 4:15), and his Holy Spirit is the Great Comforter. And 1 Peter 5:7 is still true: "Cast all your anxiety on him because he cares for you."

Singleness has its advantages. You're probably thinking about something different than I am about that, but Paul's words are what I have in mind here:

> I would like you to be free from concern. An unmarried man is concerned about the Lord's affairs—how he can please the Lord. But a married man is concerned about the affairs of this world—how he can please his wife—and his interests are divided. An unmarried woman or virgin is concerned about the Lord's affairs: Her aim is to be devoted to the Lord in both body and spirit. But a married woman is concerned about the affairs of this world—how she can please her husband. I am saying this for your own good, not

to restrict you, but that you may live in a right way in undivided devotion to the Lord (1 Cor. 7:32–35).

There are wonderful benefits to having a family, but those benefits also bring distractions to one's ministry. They divide your interests, and sometimes this means that you can't be as devoted to the work of God as you would like to be. The single person, however, is not so distracted. In fact, a devoted single can make up for the married person who has other important responsibilities conflicting with his or her ministry. A wise single will realize that God knows everybody's status and that he has a divine purpose in each circumstance. He needs some people who will serve with undivided interests.

You have an important ministry. Singles offer a great contribution to the church of today. Not just in that they can serve without distraction, but that virtually no ministry is closed to the single person. The unmarried people in our congregation do not come just to be ministered to; they come to minister, to serve others, as did the Lord Jesus (Mark 10:45). Perhaps the greatest source of personal identity for the single is serving in the local church. It can relieve frustration and fill empty time with something eternally meaningful. It is in the setting of ministering to others that relationships are built and friends are made who can lift us when we are down. Pity the one who has "no one to help him up." And you don't have to be single to be in that lonely predicament!

15

Adult Adolescence

*So then, banish anxiety from your heart and cast off the
troubles of your body, for youth and vigor are meaningless* (Eccles. 11:10).

Was the insightful Ecclesiastes preacher
prophetic, or was mid-life crisis as big a deal in his day as it
is in ours? Because look at that verse. If that doesn't fit
middle age today, I'll use Grecian Formula on my sprinkles
of gray. The troubles of your body, indeed!

Yesterday I began a rather modest exercise program to
begin whipping my body into shape after this past winter's
hibernation. Not only does it fail to perform like it used
to, but my poor body has a tough time recuperating. Today I
am reminded of muscles I forgot I had by their in-
convenient cries of pain. From limb to limb my body
groans, awaiting the adoption of a new resolution that my
brain will never force it to exercise again. "Cast off the
troubles of your body," whispers the demon of blimps and
bulges, "for your youth and vigor are long gone."

Mid-life crisis, however, involves a great deal more than
physiological changes. It's sort of like going through adolescence a second time around. Except this time puberty is not
the hitch, bewilderment *is*. Once again the body is going

through a metamorphosis, but this time the shift is downward. Like Erma Bombeck has said, "I still have everything I had twenty years ago, but it's all six inches lower." And some mental gears are shifting, too. During this "adult adolescence," a man is often hit with the desire to escape from his humdrum life, and a woman wants to reevaluate her priorities. In some ways, the teenager within you gets a resurrection.

Gail Sheehy divides up the adult developmental eras in her popular book *Passages* in this way:

1. "Pulling up Roots"—18 to 22
2. "The Trying Twenties"—22 to 28
3. "Passage to Thirties"—28 to 32
4. "Rooting and Extending"—32 to 39
5. "Deadline Decade"—35 to 45
6. "Renewal or Resignation"—after 45

The big evaluation period comes sometime during the Deadline Decade. This one is far more intense than the teenage trauma and even more jolting than the settling-down period around age thirty. Jim Conway, a man we should be very thankful for because of his valuable books on mid-life, writes in *Men in Mid-Life Crisis:* "Of all the stages and transitions a man goes through in adulthood, it appears that the mid-life crisis is the most dangerous and painful for him, his family, and the community."

While other books are fully dedicated to the turmoil, disruption, and dramatic change of the Deadline Decade, my interest is in how it relates to frustration and bouncing back. Mid-life may be the most exasperating experience of all, because it conspires with several of the other frustrators we've discussed in other chapters. Forty is a popular time for getting especially fed up with routine (chapter 1) and also a time when self-esteem perks up with questions like, "Who am I? Do I want to continue being who I am?" (chapter 2). It's a time of ditching relationships (chapter 4), which can mean that home and marriage are under their greatest threat (chapters 5 and 6). At mid-life, money and financial responsibilities become an ultimate pain in the neck (chapter 7), "success" seems totally relative (chapter 8), and stress goes off the Richter Scale (chapter 9). For many mid-lifers, batting .300 against temptation doesn't seem nearly as exciting as striking out (chapter 10), and contentment heads south for winter (chapter 12). It's a time when death and grief bring home the pale reality that life itself is fragile and passes like a vapor (chapter 13), so sometimes playing solitaire doesn't seem like such a bad idea (chapter 14).

Features of Mid-Life for Men

Peculiar things begin to happen to the man approaching middle age. He becomes engrossed with a soliloquy about his world:

"Do you like your life?" *I don't know.*

"But are you satisfied with it?" *Yes. Well, no. Well, I guess I am. I think I am.*

"You mean you like your job?" *Not exactly.*

"And look at you. Why, you've gained twenty-five extra pounds." *I know.*

"But consider your nice family, comfortable home, and decent salary." *Yeah, consider that. My wife's more interested in grocery coupons than a good time in bed. My kids are absorbed with homework they think I don't understand and activities they think I'm too old to enjoy. My comfortable home needs a new roof, a paint job, and new carpet, which my decent salary can't afford.*

"Did you see that sexy-looking woman in line at the pharmacy yesterday? I think she was giving you the eye." *Yeah.*

"And how about that young woman who just started working near your department. You'd better get acquainted." *Ha!*

"You'd better lose those twenty-five pounds first." *But I'm married.*

"See there, you are tied down. How does it feel to be tied down?" *Responsible.*

"Does that feel good? Because if you want to feel good, you'd better hurry. You'll be getting old pretty soon." *I can't let my family down.*

"Why not? They let you down all the time." *Maybe.*

The war is just beginning. Later come feelings of utter failure, perhaps a drastic career change, deep despair, perhaps severe depression, and rebellion. Gradually a man might come to appreciate how one mid-lifer viewed his state: "If I had my life to live over again, I'd be a failure. I'd be better off, because then I wouldn't have as much to lose as I do now."

Features of Mid-Life for Women

Women experience emotions somewhat different from their male counterparts'. But like men, women are absorbed with reevaluation. They are perhaps more worried about their bodies. Youthful firmness has become a thing of the past, and anti-aging formulas are working double time on the chin, neck, and eyes. Each woman's experience is slightly different, but the similarities remain.

A woman at mid-life has to admit she's getting older. Difficult as it is, she must also admit that many of the changes caused by her aging are neither attractive nor convenient. In a world of beauty queens and skin creams, that's a blow to her self-esteem. But that's where the similarities to a man's mid-life crisis take a different direction.

While menopause is still ahead of her, a woman is likely to become more future-oriented. She may enroll in night classes at a local junior college to prepare for a new career. Or she may enter the work world for the first time since giving birth to her first child. Aerobics will slim down her "older woman" image, perhaps attracting younger men and further stimulating her already renewed sexual appetite. Meanwhile, her husband is either caught up in the rat race or is overly self-indulged in his own mid-life crisis.

She has many fears besetting her: growing old, becoming a mother-in-law and grandma, losing her husband to a younger woman or death, having a hysterectomy, facing an empty, quiet nest. She feels she must bustle with energy to keep up. (Keep up with what, she's not sure.) This is the teenage girl in her coming back to life again. It's what Judith Viorst refers to in her indispensable volume, *How Did I Get to Be 40 and Other Atrocities:*

> And I'm working all day and I'm working all night
> To be good-looking, healthy, and wise.
> And adored.
> And contented.
> And brave.
> And well-read.
> And a marvelous hostess,
> Fantastic in bed,
> And bilingual,
> Athletic,
> Artistic . . .
> Won't someone please stop me?

Survival or AWOL?

There are many gurus on this subject, and I do not aspire to become one of them. Suffice it to say, there are some healthy survivors of the mid-life crisis, and others simply bug out. No one seems to know why. Probably because there is no single cut-and-dried reason.

God wants you to know there is *hope*. Just as puberty is a stage, so is mid-life. But beware of becoming "over-righteous" (see the next chapter) or you may fall into the worst of all middle-age traps: believing that good Christians don't have problems like this. Until it happens to you!

Before I share what may serve as some helpful ideas for remaining strong during this transition, let me say that most of it is unoriginal. None of it is fancy. It's not high-powered psychology. In fact, it's plain common sense. So common that you probably already thought of it and dismissed it, thinking that complex problems require complex solutions. Wrong. Make use of these things—and of other wise ideas God gives you—to combat this monster frustrator:

1. *Good health habits.* Honest, this is not a plug for the AMA. I know it sounds like something a doctor would say, but it's still true. The combination of good foods, regular exercise, and plenty of sleep not only helps the body but breeds a healthy mind. And your mind is the war ground. If it's fatigued, you can't cope—and then you're dead meat. That's not a very polite way of saying it, but it emphasizes the point.

2. *Communicate.* You're not the only one in this vacuum. Your spouse is there, too. "Yeah," you say, "she's the one holding the suction hose." Or "He's the one snoring in the recliner." It may seem that way some days, but you must gradually open up to one another. It's the only way to grow through it gracefully. Remember Browning's adage: "Come grow old along with me! The best is yet to be." Share your feelings and, when this time period is over, you'll understand the meaning behind that sage verse.

3. *Confide.* The wounds of a friend are sweet. They're tough, too. A truly confidential friend can be a God-send. The probing and prayer support he or she gives can help you make it through. One of a mid-lifer's most helpful anchors is a trustworthy person who listens without condemning. As terrible as being open about your feelings may seem, it can be a wonderful relief to have a friend to confide in.

4. *Expand.* Growth is what you want, anyway. And this is it, your deadline. Tomorrow can bring either renewal or

retirement from life itself. Launch out with what you have now and seek God's guidance on making a possible change. Don't drown yourself by using a boat full of holes, but don't sulk on the shoreline either. And make this charge at new challenges a team effort that includes your loved ones. You'll need the support of spouse, family, and friends.

5. *Learn.* Before you play football with mid-life, do some scouting. He has a powerful offense that must be understood to be defended against. Careful, or you'll have cleat marks on your face. I highly recommend reading the works of Jim and Sally Conway, as well as other fine books on the subject.

Oh, yes, and don't forget God. Psalm 77:5–6 is a reminder that he's the one who's carrying you:

> I thought about the former days,
>   the years of long ago;
> I remembered my songs in the night.
> My heart mused and my spirit inquired.

16

Thoughts on Being Overrighteous

Do not be overrighteous, neither be overwise—why destroy yourself? (Eccles. 7:16).

Today's disciples have something in common with Pavlov's dog: we've learned a trained response. And that response is usually serious. Presented with a situation that calls for opinion or judgment, we frequently try to drive all our nails with one sharp blow. We are prone to jump the gun and fire off bull's-eye shots from fifty yards or more. Then we congratulate ourselves inwardly for wisely discharging our nicely memorized codes and traditions, designed to catch all loopholes and answer all riddles.

We know there are gray areas. We admit there are gray areas and know better than to believe in a black-or-white-only approach to things. And yet, when someone gets into the gray that we think is black, the overrighteous part of us waters at the mouth, eager to give a response. Mr. (or Mrs.) Righteous has learned that with "perfect discernment" comes a tasty morsel: the inward gratification of feeling incredibly spiritual. After licking away the saliva from his truly holy lips, this super saint within our bosom lies down in the corner until someone who was supposed to stay in the white gets into the gray.

That's the bad part. Here's the worst part: we practice this witch-medicine spirituality on ourselves. Our faith can become an exact science to us. For too many of us it is neatly categorized, well rehearsed, and—dare we admit it?—a trifle boring. Some of you won't 'fess up, because you don't want to hear your Pavlovian taskmaster drive you to penance. No, not a hundred "Hail Mary's." Instead, we pray more, give more, and do more. Doesn't it matter that we're becoming conventional, trapped, exhausted, joyless, tight Christians? We're in desperate need of rediscovering the joy of our salvation (Ps. 51:12)—as soon as we can convince the rest of the world to be 100 percent sure of theirs.

Don't get me wrong. I believe aimlessness is disastrous for believers. Worldliness has danced with the church long enough to weaken her spirit. I'm not downing a genuine pursuit of God or a reverential lifting up of his holiness. It's the short-circuited idea that "God's on the other side of the universe, and I'm in charge" I'm opposed to. Some call it Pharisaism, others call it lopsidedness. But, in the language of frustration, it's the problem of being overrighteous.

In *Man's Search for Meaning*, Victor Frankl describes the real saint as one who knew nothing about sainthood. He writes: "If he actually tried to be righteous for the sake of having a good conscience, he would become a Pharisee and cease to be a truly moral person. I think that even saints did not care for anything other than simply to serve God, and I doubt that they even had it in mind to become saints. If that were the case, they would have become only perfectionists rather than saints." Now there's a serious thought for believers who are on a quest for total holiness.

Embarrassing Memories

I am a member of Super Saints Anonymous. Yes, it's tough to say that, but it's true. I once was drunk with the need to be on a pedestal, to have the glamorous recognition of being one of the "answer men," to have the capability to nail even Jell-o to the wall. Everyone fell under my scrutiny, and precious few escaped my criticism.

You name it: whatever the wild, hyper-religious eccentricity, I believed in it. Hair off the ears and collar was a must to walk with the giants. All secular tunes were forbidden from my music cabinet and everyone else's, too. White was white, black was black, and gray was "compromise," which was the cardinal sin.

What was compromise? Compromise was a woman wearing slacks for any reason, or someone using any other Bible version except the King James. Compromise was associating with any church or organization not accepted within our circles. Compromise was mixed swimming, or attending a movie theater, no matter how decent the film.

I had it all figured out. Except for one problem: my answers didn't satisfy even me. I kept telling myself they were biblical—for a while. When I grew enough spiritually to recognize the discrepancies, I was ashamed.

Why ashamed? Not because of error, although that was bad enough. I used to sit and recall the dumb things I had said and done to people who wouldn't conform to my dictates of "religiosity," and my face literally burned with red embarrassment. To some I had done irreparable damage. How could I ever apologize? How would I ever explain my drastic change of philosophy? What could be done to reverse the effect of my words on the choice of others to believe the same dogmas? The shame and guilt were hard to shake, but finally I was on the wagon. So was my super-saint status.

The Celebration of Grace

Robert Capon beautifully describes the pleasure of being free from the frustrating grip of overrighteousness in his work *Between Noon and Three:*

Indeed, grace is the celebration of life, relentlessly hounding all the noncelebrants of the world. It is a floating cosmic bash shouting its way through the streets of the universe, flinging the sweetness of its cassations to every window, pounding at every door in a hilarity beyond all liking and happening, until the prodigals come out at last and dance and the elder brothers finally take their fingers out of their ears.

Guess who "the elder brothers" are? Right. They are us, and that isn't very pretty. But it does bring to light another dark alley of frustration: it's nerve-racking to be "perfect." For we look about us at "sinners" enjoying God's party, and we cry in true elder-brother fashion: "Look! All these years I've been slaving for you and never disobeyed your orders. Yet you never gave me even a young goat so I could celebrate with my friends. But when this son of yours who has squandered your property with prostitutes comes home, you kill the fattened calf for him!" (Luke 15:29–30). Did you catch his frustration? "Never disobeyed your orders." That's what loyalty had become to him—*orders.* And that adds up to frustration.

This happens to us when we become brazen, suspicious, somber, and overscrupulous. It's what A. W. Tozer called "religious melancholy." Charles Spurgeon took up the humorous pen of his pseudonym, John Ploughman, to impart these words of reminder:

> The most careful driver one day upsets the cart, the cleverest cook spills a little broth, and as I know to my sorrow a very decent ploughman will now and then break the plough, and often make a crooked furrow. . . . The best wine has its lees. All men's faults are not written on their foreheads, and it's quite as well they are not, or hats would need very wide brims.

Confession is the beginning of relief from over-righteousness. But I guess one must first recognize it in himself. Perhaps this is why Jesus reserved his harshest words for the deeply religious people. In spite of their pious sincerity, Jesus scalded them with stinging words. As long as they could not recognize their own sin, they could not receive his grace and forgiveness. Severe confrontation was their only hope. Otherwise they were destined to carry the frustration of guilt and thus miss out on the celebration. Unfortunately, they kept their fingers in their ears.

In *Come to the Party*, Karl Olsson writes: "Nowhere does our independence of God glow so fiercely as in our goodness. When desire for perfection drives us into moral scrupulousness or even into self-effacing benevolence, we feel with Milton's Eve 'divinity within us breeding wings.'"

Therefore, it is critical that, once we see the problem and identify the frustration within ourselves, we then allow our humanity to live. No, no, not sinning that grace may abound! Just bringing our fears and doubts and inadequacies before the Lord.

What I'm talking about is doing away with super saintdom. Letting gray really be gray. Taking your fingers out of your ears.

17

Justice Revisited

And I saw something else under the sun: In the place of judgment—wickedness was there, in the place of justice— wickedness was there (Eccles. 3:16).

I used to have complete confidence in the American judicial system. Not anymore. I've seen too many contradictions firsthand. Politics. Plea-bargaining. Probations. Paroles. Perjury. Publicity. Paralysis. Unfortunately, I'm one of those poor buzzards who must settle for complaining, because the machinery has become too complicated for my oversimplified ideas of legal justice. And yet, I can relate to the careful, observant eye of Mr. Ecclesiastes.

A few years ago I was physically assaulted at the scene of an accident for trying to call a police officer. The man who crashed into my new car had no auto insurance, and he wanted to just call the damages even. My polite efforts at doing the right thing nearly got me killed. Literally! I received a horizontal fracture across the bridge of my nose, a grotesque split from my earlobe to my inner ear, bruised ribs, and other serious contusions.

When I gave the police a description of the man who assaulted me, they immediately knew who it was because of his notorious record. After months of refusing to obey his subpoena, the man was finally arrested to stand trial. He faced four charges, three of them felonies. His sentence? Three days in jail and a $300 fine.

"I paid more in insurance deductibles than he did in fines," I said sharply to the prosecutor, once we were outside the courtroom.

"The judge expects you to sue him," he responded.

"Why?" I was incredulous.

"That's the way the system works. If you want further punishment and damages, take out a civil suit. Be sure your insurance company will."

"I don't have the time to chase this guy around courtrooms for the next two years. Besides, I'd probably never see a penny of it anyway. Why didn't the judge just put him in jail and make him pay for all the damage he caused?" I was irate.

"Look, I've got another case to try. Get a lawyer and sue for the damages," said the already-beaten district attorney as he turned the corner.

Suddenly I was glad I hadn't become the lawyer I had aspired to be in college. The system would have ruined me. My first encounter with the judicial process left me cold. Several descriptive words ran through my head on that day, those which I cannot write here. It was difficult to ask God to forgive me for my subsequent malice and anger.

Since then, I have had the unpleasant task of being a witness and/or complainant in other criminal cases. At other times I have had the difficult ministry of standing with the victims of serious crimes. And I must tell you, what I have seen has made me sick. I watched an attorney help his young defendant lie because of a technicality. The boy walked away from a grand-larceny charge, snickering at the victims. Less than a month later, he was a repeat offender. Before my eyes, pedophiles have gone free, sexual abusers of minors have received mere probation, perjurers have barely received a warning, and a child murderer was nearly paroled.

It's a sin and a shame, but—in the place of justice— wickedness *is* there. What a frustration! Listen, there are few like it. Unless you've been a victim, you probably don't understand how deep the pain of injustice goes. The bitterness is hard to fight. When all of your life you were taught to respect law and order, it's a shock to find that the law has become disorderly and does more to protect the criminal than the victim. If a matter ever gets to court, after it's all said and done, there is rarely a feeling of justice for the victim. The penalties are frequently light and such a long time in coming. (Unless the IRS is after a tax offender.)

This is what the cynical preacher referred to in his further analysis of justice: "When the sentence for a crime is not quickly carried out, the hearts of the people are filled with schemes to do wrong" (Eccles. 8:11).

Praise the Lord! God's justice isn't like man's. That truth alone has inspired me to bounce back from more than one heartache. Although it matters to us what our fellowman does about crimes committed against us, what God says and does is what matters most. His courtroom is the highest of all, and true everlasting justice always prevails there.

He hears every case. Our courts don't. They can't. There's just too much crime, and too many gripes in our "sue 'em" society. The courtroom has degenerated into a sort of judicial lottery where plaintiffs try to win big. Real justice often gets lost in the shuffle. Not with God. You can always take your case before him. "The LORD is known by his justice; the wicked are ensnared by the work of their hands" (Ps. 9:16).

Let it be a source of comfort that you can plead your case to the God of justice, and he hears every cry. God sees the tears you shed. Man's court may have failed you, or man's law, but God will never let you down. While his judgment may not come for months or years, and you may not see it

or hear of it, his justice can flow with a fury. Be thankful
you don't have to carry thoughts of revenge: "For the LORD
is a God of justice. Blessed are all who wait for him!" (Isa.
30:18b).

His penalties are severe. We have drifted away from old-
fashioned truths like Hebrews 10:31: "It is a dreadful thing
to fall into the hands of the living God." So many people
have no fear of God before their eyes. Until we begin judgment at the household of faith, with a serious sense of
justice about our own acts of unrighteousness, we are in
pretty poor shape to expect holy punishment upon the in-
justices done to us. However, when a man loves mercy and
longs to live justly, woe to the one who brings him hurt.
Whether man's system vindicates him or not, God will. Far
better would it be for a criminal if man's system caught
him and chastised him terribly than to owe the Almighty
for an injustice committed against one of his children.
Mark these sage words: "Fear the LORD and the king, my
son, and do not join with the rebellious, for those two will
send sudden destruction upon them, and who knows what
calamities they can bring?" (Prov. 24:21–22).

He has a perfect balance of mercy. We mortals do not.
Being created in the image of God gives us a strong sense of
justice, but sometimes that trait is tainted by our sin
nature. For instance, people get involved in marches and
movements because their sense of justice is violated. Some
people also have such a sensitive spirit of mercy that they
sometimes forget the importance of fairness and consistency. God is not given to such imbalances. He is both
perfectly just and generously merciful. As Micah 6:8
says: "He has showed you, O man, what is good. And what
does the LORD require of you? To act justly and to love
mercy. . . ."

He heals the victim. When I accompanied the family of a
daughter who had been sexually victimized to report the
crime, I felt a deep sense of remorse for the girl whose
innocence had been taken from her at such a young age. As

I observed the indescribable pain the whole family was feeling, I wondered if any of them would ever fully recover from the nightmare of what had happened. After a few minutes of waiting, an attractive young woman came into the room and went out alone with the girl. The curiosity of what was going on made the matter seem like an endless ordeal. Weeks later, when the court system dismissed the issue with a simple probation, my disillusionment swelled pregnant with disbelief. And yet, one consolation lingered: what I had learned about the young woman who had talked to the abused child. She was a victim's advocate. In fact, she herself had been molested as a young girl and had chosen her career in order to touch the lives of girls and women who meet with a catastrophe like hers. Her influence had been significant in this case. God used her tremendously. Subsequently the young victim I accompanied received a wonderful healing of her memories. Gradually she came to forgive the one who had abused her. Today, God has given her the grace to use the evil that came into her life to minister good into the lives of others.

He never forgets. "For he who avenges blood remembers; he does not ignore the cry of the afflicted" (Ps. 9:12). Several years ago, the brother of a woman in our church was serving as a police officer. Little did he know how famous his story would become as he drove his beat one night. When he saw a man come out of a convenience grocery store late that night, something about the scene looked suspicious. He went to question the man, but before he got there it was apparent a crime was in progress. Stepping out of his car, he called for the man to halt. Suddenly he was wounded by an unexpected shot from the man's hidden weapon. The officer fell to the pavement in pain and surprise. What happened next made shocking headlines. The criminal approached the wounded officer and emptied his gun into his body.

Miraculously, the officer survived. Newspapers told of the awful crime. People cried for justice. The villain was finally captured and sentenced to prison. However, in a mere three years, he was released on parole. Unbelievable? Shocking? Outrageous? Yes. And to this day the officer's family and friends grapple with feelings of revenge. They wonder about our system of legal and criminal justice. I can sympathize with them, because it baffles me how quickly the rights of victims and their families are forgotten.

God never forgets. The tears of the afflicted are ever before him. In healing them, he also vindicates them. Just because jail doors sometimes swing open to freedom does not mean all is forgotten. Society's idea of paying a debt is coming to be less than enough to satisfy God. So, as far as he is concerned, many criminals are still fugitives from justice—justice that he will administer.

When I revisit the holy nature of God, a new sense of security and confidence sweeps over me. Man's system may fail, but God is just, merciful, and faithful (Matt. 23:23). And, one day, I will learn of how he overruled in many of the cases that bother me today.

18

Never a Still Moment

Better one handful with tranquillity than two handfuls with toil and chasing after the wind (Eccles. 4:6).

The sun had gone down when I arrived home the other day, and dusk was setting in. It had been a long, long day. I had planned on taking half of the day off, but one situation piled onto another, and I was busy into the late afternoon. As I picked up the newspaper in the driveway, I noticed my eight-year-old son, Jared, gathering up his soccer goalmarkers.

"How's it going, buddy?" I called to him as I walked toward the garage.

No reply.

"Hey! How are you doing?" I tried again.

With a frown and a glare he turned and sounded back, "You're late. You promised to play soccer with me today. Where were you?"

"Well," I hesitated, full of guilt because I had forgotten my promise, "things just got busier and busier at the church."

"They always do, Dad. You're always late."

"That's not true." I tried not to be defensive with my tone, because I could see that Jared was about to cry. At that moment I hated myself. I hated my job. His dejection was crushing me. I had let him down. He needed me and had counted on me, and I had let him down. Every caring parent has experienced the emptiness that enveloped me as I stood looking into my little boy's angry eyes.

"Oh, yes, it is true! You're always talking to somebody. We stay late after church. People call you on the phone. But you don't keep your promises to me." Now he had the knife in my heart, turning it.

"You're right." I couldn't believe my ears. Or my mouth. What? A child counseling his father? Out of the mouths of babes and sucklings. . . .

Jared just stood there, probably stunned by my answer: "I'm sorry I disappointed you, and I'm sorry I've become too busy. Will you forgive me?"

While my son is a tough communicator, he has a tender heart. "Yes, I forgive you," he said and then added after a cautious pause, "but will you start remembering your promises?"

"I will do my best, son," I answered, fearful of what circumstance would beg to interfere next time. "If you'll let me, I'd like to make up for not being home when I said I would be."

"How?" It appeared as if nothing could replace missing soccer.

"How about a two-out-of-three chess match?"

"Yeah!" The excitement flooded over him.

Still, the situation menaced me in bed that night. I didn't sleep well. God's Spirit searched my priorities up and down. Then *I* did. Then he did again. "This cannot happen anymore," I told myself. "This business of being over-committed must stop. This incident with Jared today must be the turning point. . . ." The self-lecturing continued into the night.

Don't worry. This isn't another round of the latest literature on the popular theme of burnout. It isn't the prelude to another sermon on Workaholics Anonymous, either.

However, Chuck Swindoll's words on fatigue bear repeating:

> We've been programmed to think that fatigue is next to godliness. That the more exhausted we are (and look!), the more spiritual we are and the more we earn God's smile of approval. We bury all thoughts of enjoying life . . . for those who are really committed Christians are those who work, work, work. And preferably, with great intensity. As a result, we have become a generation of people who worship our work . . . who work at our play . . . and who play at our worship.

Ouch! That stings. I've been there, and I know what it means to need an injection of time for my calendar. So many of us have become victims of the I-can't-say-no syndrome. Before we know it, we're in over our heads with no feasible way out. We find ourselves trying to handle more than enough for three without enough nerves or energy for even one. It reminds me of the poor fellow in this poem:

Many, many years ago when I was twenty-three
I was married to a widow who was pretty as could be.
This widow had a grown-up daughter who had hair of red,
My father fell in love with her and soon they two were wed.

This made my dad my son-in-law and changed my very life.
My daughter was my mother, for she was my father's wife.
To complicate the matter, even though it brought me joy;
I soon became the father of a bouncing baby boy.

This little baby then became a brother-in-law to dad,
Which made him then my uncle, though it made me very sad.
My wife became my mother's mother and it makes me blue;
For although she's my wife, that means she's my grandmother, too.

Now if my wife's my grandmother, then I am her grandchild,
And everytime I think of it, it nearly drives me wild.
For I have just become the strangest case you ever saw—
As husband of my grandmother—*I am my own grandpa!*

Now that's what I call overcommitted! And yet, that's what it feels like to be overcommitted—like being your own grandpa. That's what the preacher of Ecclesiastes was getting at when he said, "Better one handful with tranquillity than two handfuls with toil and chasing after the wind" (Eccles. 4:6).

Overcommitment is a master frustrator. It not only robs you of leisure time, but it invades your personal life. Overinvolvement, though not a problem in the least for some Christians (because they barely know what involvement is), gradually leads its prey away from the path of delight and down to the altar to become a burnt offering. *Bulletin:* Until you give yourself permission to say no, you'll constantly be trying to get fire out of ashes.

By remembering to ask ourselves three simple questions, we can put to rest our areas of overinvolvement:

Why am I doing what I'm doing? Many people allow themselves to get swamped because they equate worth with accomplishment. The more they do, the better they are. To them, the goal of their involvement has something to do with being needed. What these champions of "too many irons in the fire" do not realize is the subtlety of what drives them on. It's a hard thing to earn one's own self-esteem.

Someone has said that we humans are strange: we run faster when we lose our way. What we're starved for is a feast of blessed quietness: "Be still, and know that I am God . . ." (Ps. 46:10). That doesn't mean laziness. Just a peaceful inquiry at the throne of God about whether or not taking on yet another task is *his* will. Or is it really mine, because it somehow gives me a sense of gratification? Motives and goals are a problem for the overcommitted. Beneath it all, a violation of these twin thermometers of ambition is what turns up the heat of frustration.

Am I leaving the more important things undone? Foolish is the man who saves the whole world while his family goes to hell. God really used Jared's soccer sermon to get hold of me. The lesson I learned is good for all people: I can't be all things to all people at all times. Not if the truly important things are truly important. Pray tell, if our families are the priority we say they are, then why are we in three sports leagues? Why does the T.V. smile when you push its off button? Why are you a deacon, and a Sunday-school teacher, and a Bible-class leader, and a choir member, and a part-time usher, and head of the jail ministry, and chairman of the missions committee? Do you think God needs an assistant? Are you trying out for the Trinity? If our family relationships are second only to God, then why aren't we home more often? Psalm 37:5 tells us to commit our way to the Lord. I have a feeling if some of us did that, God would narrow our way from an eight-lane autobahn to a two-lane country road. That leads us to question number three.

Am I doing what God wants? Overinvolvement is the result of either doing what we want or the inability to say no to what others want. Whatever the case, it means something must be cut out if God's will is to be obeyed. Too many commitments is our schedule's way of warning us: "Ah, ah, ah! Instead you'd better learn to say, 'If God wants me to do this or that, I will.' Otherwise, you're gonna be spread too thin." (That's an Earles paraphrase of James 4:15). One of the hardest things you'll ever do is honestly clear your schedule of the commitments God never intended you to have and those in which he no longer wants you involved. Go ahead. Do a cut-and-paste job on your schedule.

I did, and my chess game has radically improved. Also, a soccer-coach friend of mine suggested that I get shin guards. Thanks for the sermon, son.

19

When the
Almond Tree Blossoms

. . . when the almond tree blossoms and the grasshopper drags himself along and desire no longer is stirred. Then man goes to his eternal home and mourners go about the streets (Eccles. 12:5).

What crosses your mind when you think about growing older? Are you frightened? Apprehensive? How do you feel about older people? Do you look upon them as tottering, feeble, useless, and friendless? For some, the very mention of "elderly" brings to mind old-age homes, crippling arthritis, the smell of hospitals, senility, and death. What age do you consider old? Fifty? Seventy? Ninety? And what does it mean to grow older?

Many of us would have a difficult time agreeing with Jonathan Swift, who said: "No wise man ever wished to be younger." No, we find it much easier to relate to the cartoon of the aged beauty standing before her vanity and saying: "Mirror, mirror on the wall, lie to me." We often underestimate the value of old age for its gains in wisdom and experience, viewing old age as loss. A Chinese sage named Confucius had words for us to ponder:

At 15, I applied myself to the study of wisdom.

At 30, I grew strong in it.

At 40, I no longer had doubt.

At 50, there was nothing on earth that could shake me.

At 70, I could follow the dictate of my heart without disobeying moral law.

It was this final frustration that the man of vanities inscribed in his ledger of hard-to-settle accounts—the frustration of aging. He gives a brief introduction in Ecclesiastes 12:1–2, before applying his descriptive pen in a poetic review of the prospects of growing old:

> Remember your Creator
> in the days of your youth,
> before the days of trouble come
> and the years approach
> when you will say,
> "I find no pleasure in them"—
> before the sun and the light
> and the moon and the stars grow dark,
> and the clouds return after the rain. . . .

What a heavy way to start the last section of a book! And yet, the writer reveals to us the very concerns most of us have about becoming old: boredom, depression, and a sense of obsolescence. Does it shock you to hear that last year 25 percent of all suicides involved people over the age of sixty? Would you be surprised to learn that there is a 30 percent higher mortality rate for retired people as compared to working people of the same age? You see, for many people it is a fearful, frustrating, and debilitating thing to grow old and feel like an unnecessary evil. The prospect of losing control of one's mind, bowels, and emotions is dreadful, especially when our mutual wish is that we can die with dignity.

Age-ism

Ramsey Clark said, "People who don't cherish their elderly have forgotten whence they came and whither they go." With those words he was nailing down a central problem with our society—the force of *age-ism*. That is to say, we have predetermined roles for the elderly, and we have certain social prejudices against "senior citizens."

This is a significant frustration for older people in our country. They must at once decide how they feel about a society that places such a premium on youth, vitality, and physical strength, and at the same time decide how they feel about themselves, because they grew up in that society. Perhaps it is an awareness of these very things that worries some people about growing old. It is natural for us to wonder: "Will there still be a place for me when I am old? How will I be treated? Will I be respected? Will I be forgotten?"

The ferocious stories of classic fiction may have subtlely affected some of our opinions about old age. For instance, the Grimm brothers depict age as a devilish enemy in their writings. Remember "Snow White," where a wrinkled queen wants to destroy the loveliness of youth? How about "Hansel and Gretel"? After their aging parents send them off to die, hoarding the food for themselves, the youngsters meet up with another old person who plans to eat them. In "Jew Among Thorns," the old are rich and the young are poor, and the old cheat the young. "Faithful John" has an old king manipulating things so as to dominate his son from the grave. In "The Six Servants," an old lady devises a scheme to prevent a young damsel from marrying. From these stories we gather that age is evil and must be crushed by youth. The Grimms are properly named, I think! Their perspective on aging appears to be one of disgust, implying that the young must do in the old as if they were rabid bats.

We need to hear the preaching of Cicero: "Not by physical force, not by bodily swiftness and agility, are great things accomplished, but by deliberation, authority, and judgment; qualities with which old age is abundantly provided." Or, as Leviticus 19:32 teaches us: "Rise in the presence of the aged, show respect for the elderly and revere your God. I am the LORD." A couple of other verses worth looking at are Proverbs 16:31 and 20:29.

Solomon's Poetry

Following his dark, abrupt introduction, Solomon goes into a poetical analogy of the physical frustrations of old age. Check this chart to get a feel for solomon's insight on aging's effect on the body:

Description	Analogy
"the keepers of the house tremble" (v. 3)	trembling lips
"the strong men stoop" (v. 3)	stooped legs and back
"grinders cease because they are few" (v. 3)	lose teeth (buy dentures!)
"those looking through the windows grow dim" (v. 3)	eyesight fails
"sound of grinding fades" (v. 4)	deafness sets in
"men rise up at the sound of birds" (v. 4)	insomnia
"men are afraid of heights and of danger in the streets" (v. 5)	old age brings various phobias
"the almond tree blossoms" (v. 5)	graying hair
"the grasshopper drags himself along" (v. 5)	stiff joints
"desire no longer is stirred" (v. 5)	sexual decline
"the silver cord is severed" (v. 6)	possibly referring to a stroke
"the golden bowl is broken" (v. 6)	gradual loss of memory

"the wheel broken at the well"   heart failure
(v. 6)

"dust returns to the ground" (v. 7)   death

Beyond Creativity?

The preacher of Ecclesiastes certainly was in touch with the physical anguish that frequently accompanies old age. However, his perspective is once again strikingly incomplete because of frustration's irritating presence. He leaves us with the impression that we can serve God and achieve great feats only in our youth. Not so!

It is comforting—especially as we grow older—to look at examples of remarkable old people who have created masterpieces, touched lives, made wondrous discoveries, or somehow changed the course of world history. The list could go on and on, but let me mention some of the most inspiring:

Sophocles wrote *Oedipus Rex* at 75

Goethe finished *Faust* shortly before his death at 83

Cervantes completed, at 68, what some call the greatest novel of all time, *Don Quixote*

Alfred Lord Tennyson produced poetry into his eighties

Giuseppe Verdi composed his famous *Falstaff* at age 80, and continued composing until he was 85

Galileo did his most important work in his seventies

Gandhi continued to serve his people's cause for freedom and reform until his death at 78

Picasso painted prolifically until he died at age 91

Victor Hugo finished one of his greatest works, *The Legend of the Centuries,* just in time for his eightieth birthday. At a banquet given in his honor, he said, "Gentlemen, I am eighty and I am beginning my career!" How much more could be said of Einstein, Schweitzer, Tolstoy, Shaw, Toscanini, and Stravinsky. Yes, creativity can be sustained well into the later years of life.

Maybe nobody better understands what old people can do than the West Hartford third-grader Margaret Huyck mentions in her book *Growing Older*. What a beautiful job this child did with the assignment "What Is a Grandma?":

> A Grandma is a lady who has no children of her own, so she likes other people's little boys and girls.
>
> A Grandfather is a man Grandmother. He goes for walks with the boys and they talk about fishing and things like that.
>
> Grandmas don't have to do anything except be there.
>
> They're so old they shouldn't play hard. It is enough if they drive us to the supermarket where the pretend horse is and have lots of dimes ready.
>
> Or if they take us for walks, they should slow down past things like pretty leaves or caterpillars. And they should never say "Hurry up!"
>
> Usually they are fat, but not too fat. They wear glasses and funny underwear. They can take their teeth and gums off.
>
> They don't have to be smart, only answer questions like why dogs hate cats, and how come God isn't married.
>
> They don't talk baby talk like visitors do because it is hard to understand.
>
> When they read to us they don't skip words and they don't mind if it is the same story.
>
> Grandmas are the only grownups who have got time—so everybody should have a Grandmother especially if you don't have television.

There are some common traits experienced by those who have made the passage into the last third of their lives. These characteristics, though not met by everyone in the same way, bring both pleasure and frustration to the aging process. They can also become part of the strategy for growing gracefully into a contented and still-productive old age:

1. *Change in sense of time.* Seniors usually concentrate on the quality of time left rather than the quantity, because they have much less of a need to prepare for their own future. (Elijah was intent on getting Elisha trained to replace him.)

2. *Life review.* The reminiscence of the old should not be dismissed as senility, since the process is crucial to accepting the wrinkles and changes that come with the transition into late maturity. It allows an elder to piece his life together and see what has brought him to this stage of the life cycle. (Study Job for this.)

3. *Making peace with the past.* Many people go through a life review to deal with unresolved problems of the past. One of the strategies of bouncing back from "old-ageitis" is to come to terms with past regrets. Often, in the later years, there is an impulse to atone. (Jacob is a perfect illustration.)

4. *Fondness for the familiar.* It is normal for the elderly to be attached to home, not interested in making long journeys. Other familiar things become increasingly more meaningful: pets, keepsakes, photo albums, heirlooms, scrapbooks, old letters. These are a person's links to the past, the evidence that he or she was here. (Naomi finished her life in familiar surroundings.)

5. *Desire for continuity.* The passing on of knowledge and tradition is a distinguishing mark of aging. One feels a certain compulsion to hand down the insights afforded by experience when the wisdom of years sets in. (Solomon is a good case study here.)

6. *Leaving a legacy.* Who doesn't want to hand down a heritage and be remembered after death? (Look at what David left behind.)

7. *Transmission of power.* In close families, where leadership is a key ingredient, the passing of the torch is very important. A father may wish to transfer

power and authority to a son. (Moses was careful in his selection of Joshua.)

8. *Sense of fulfillment.* Often this is a result of life review. One feels satisfaction in having survived against difficult odds. (The apostle Paul said, "I have fought the good fight, I have finished the race, I have kept the faith" [2 Tim. 4:7]).

9. *Capacity for growth.* Old age should not signify an ending, but a beginning—the unrelenting belief that there is more to be done. (Caleb still wanted mountaintop experiences, not just another tablespoon of Geritol.)

In the aging game, success is dependent upon a willingness to accept challenges and resist society's idea of old age as a time of aimless waiting. It means accepting the advancing years and facing late life with a revised blueprint for happiness. It means adapting to the aspects of old age that are not so glorious. Above all, it means reaching deep for faith for the last stretch of the road, yet always being alert to the new possibilities around the next bend.

> And the seventh sorrow
> Is the slow goodbye
> Of the face with its wrinkles that
>   looks through the window
> As the year packs up
> Like a tatty fairground
> That came for the children.
>   *Ted Hughes*
>   *Season Songs*

"Behold, I will create new heavens and a new earth. . . . Never again will there be in it an infant who lives but a few days, or an old man who does not live out his years; he who dies at a hundred will be thought a mere youth; he who fails to reach a hundred will be thought accursed" (Isa. 65:17a, 20).

20

Go Ahead—Make Your Day!

Whatever your hand finds to do, do it with all your might . . . (Eccles. 9:10).

Mankind's outlook is often so futile, so pessimistic. We tend to build on our hurts rather than our hopes, which stifles our ambition to enter the Land of Beginning-Again. The tyranny of life's frustrations sometimes imprisons us. Instead of learning to laugh at the weird idiosyncrasies of life, we take them all too seriously. The result is: we don't attempt some things we should because we're exasperated with life, and what things we do attempt often come short because our irritability prevents us from doing our best.

It reminds me of the tourist who walked down a pier and saw a fisherman pull in a large fish, measure its length, and throw it back in. When he caught a second fish, a bit shorter, he put it on his stringer. For several minutes the fisherman caught fish, measured them, and threw back the big ones. Finally, the onlooker's curiosity got the best of him, and he questioned the angler, "Excuse me, but why do you keep the little ones and throw away the big ones?" The leathery fellow shrugged and answered without hesitation, "Because my frying pan is only ten inches across."

How many of us act as if we think with that kind of logic? Our problems are viewed as defeating, not challenging. Impasses are seen as impossibilities, not opportunities. Trials are accepted as barriers, not hurdles. We choose the easy path because we fear what awaits us on the hard one. I am reminded again and again of Dr. Bob Jones, Sr.'s, words: "The test of a man's character is what it takes to stop him."

Develop a Strategy

What we really need is an organized plan for solving frustration when it comes. Here are some ideas:

Expect frustration. Think ahead. Spot possible irritations before they come. Don't just enthusiastically rush into a situation without considering the potential kinks. Ignoring the thought that problems may arise is a main reason why people get frustrated—they weren't realistic about their well-intentioned ideas. Challenge-seekers know there are flaws in practically every plan. They ask themselves, "What's wrong with this? What might go wrong?" Then they solve those snags ahead of time. That's a sure way to head off frustration at the pass.

Thrive on problems. "These [trials] have come so that your faith—of greater worth than gold, which perishes even though refined by fire—may be proved genuine and may result in praise, glory and honor when Jesus Christ is revealed" (1 Peter 1:7). Those who learn to feed on difficulties become tomorrow's frustration-busters. If obstacles aren't tackled, whatever the cost, decay sets in and warps, pilfers, and spoils the best of plans. To the opposite degree, the will to fight back against the intimidation of defeat brings strength, hope, and courage. The greatest of these is hope.

Welcome irritations. What? Have I gone mad? Dealing with them is one thing, but *welcoming* them? Ridiculous! No, not really. The best lessons are not learned during soft times, but during hard ones. The absence of frustration is not nearly so important as our reaction to it when it is present. Though Jesus does call the heavy-laden and gives them rest, he also places his yoke upon them (Matt. 11:28–30). His yoke is easy and his burden is light, but he places it upon us nonetheless. Then we are told in Galatians 6:5 ". . . each one should carry his own load." Bearing our burdens is a lot like pumping iron; it makes us stronger. A refusal to face our struggles is a guarantee that we will continue in our weaknesses.

Don't let frustration steer you wrong. This is the devil's desire. If he can confuse you, upset you, disappoint you, humiliate you, and hurt you, then maybe he can turn you. That's how he thinks. Since he can't sit on God's throne in heaven, he'll do all he can to sit on God's throne in your life. And, if he can't sit there, he'll be satisfied to convince you to sit there. He is pleased when you throw up your hands in agony and disgust, for he imagines it won't be long before he makes you his footstool. Decide now: "I will not do wrong, whatever the pressures." Double-check your resources. Admit your weakness to God. Call for his help and lay your heartaches in his hands. He cares for you.

Identify frustrations when they come. Matters can get out of hand quickly. Before we know it, problems appear to be "unsolvable." How suddenly the problem between Paul and Barnabas escalated! All because of Paul's frustration with John Mark's early departure for home on their first missionary journey (Acts 15:36–40). Stubbornly, Paul and Barnabas broke company and went separate ways. Isn't it odd how quickly their sharp disagreement became so complex? We can avoid similar results by marking our frustrations when they break out and dealing with them immediately.

Ask for help. One of the secrets of discipleship is teamwork. No disciple is an island in the world. Rather, he belongs to a body, to a network of supporters. Again, we read in Galatians: "Carry each other's burdens, and in this way you will fulfill the law of Christ" (6:2). It is not to our praise that many of us are too proud to admit that we need

help. We are too much like a little girl who resists her
mother's assistance and says, "No Mommy, I do it myself!"
Pity those who haven't enough backbone to pick up their
burden, who only whine about it. But pity, too, those who
insist on carrying their burdens alone, who miss the beauty
of Christian love.

Consider Your Blessings

The focus of this volume has been on the major frustrations of life. My goal has been to encourage you; to relate to
you through the common experiences we share; to get you
to laugh at some aspects of your trials. I want to help you
believe in yourself enough to keep on keeping on and to
inspire your faith in God, who desires more than anyone
else to help you turn your obstacles into opportunities. I
have tried to lighten your load a bit—to burn off some of
the fog that blocks your way.

There is no surefire remedy for frustration. Sometimes it
is funny; sometimes it is crushing. It was not my intent to
delude you in any way, for in this life there will be tribula-
tion.

And yet, we must never forget our blessings. We are
skilled at this—forgetting. Like the children of Israel, we
drink from the rock, we eat the manna and the quail, and
we enjoy the guidance of the Cloud, but when it gets hot in
the kitchen, we volunteer to return to Egypt. A bad memory is the curse of a would-be disciple. He can't remember
enough to keep him following the Way.

We can't vaccinate ourselves against frustration. There
can be no immunity. But we can remain thankful for our
blessings. In doing that, we are apt to stay true.

> To him who is able to keep you from falling and to pre-
> sent you before his glorious presence without fault and with
> great joy—to the only God our Savior be glory, majesty,

power and authority, through Jesus Christ our Lord, before all ages, now and forevermore! Amen (Jude 24–25).

So don't be afraid to buy a larger frypan. A bigger catch may bring tougher trials, but it brings greater blessings, too. Go ahead—bounce back—make your day!